PURSUING
POSTDEPENDENCY
POLITICS

PURSUING POSTDEPENDENCY POLITICS

South-South Relations in the Caribbean

H. Michael Erisman

Lynne Rienner Publishers ■ Boulder & London

Published in the United States of America in 1992 by
Lynne Rienner Publishers, Inc.
1800 30th Street, Boulder, Colorado 80301

and in the United Kingdom by
Lynne Rienner Publishers, Inc.
3 Henrietta Street, Covent Garden, London WC2E 8LU

Library of Congress Cataloging-in-Publication Data
   Pursuing postdependency politics : South-South relations in the
Caribbean / H. Michael Erisman.
      p. cm.
   Includes bibliographical references and index.
   ISBN 1-55587-078-3 (hc)
      1. Caribbean Area—Foreign relations—1945– 2. Caribbean
Community. 3. Caribbean Area—Dependency on foreign countries.
4. Caribbean Area—Economic integration. I. Title.
F2183.E75 1992
327.729—dc20   92-19097
                                                               CIP

British Cataloguing in Publication Data
A Cataloguing in Publication record for this book
is available from the British Library.

Printed and bound in the United States of America

The paper used in this publication meets the requirements
of the American National Standard for Permanence of
Paper for Printed Library Materials Z39.48-1984.

Contents

Illustrations

Tables

Figures

Preface

Central to the human condition, in its collective as well as its individual expressions, are both retrospection and anticipation—a dual process of looking at where we have come from and where we may be going. In many instances these two exercises are unrelated; they are undertaken at different times and often by different people working essentially in isolation from one another. But for Latin America in general and the Caribbean in particular, 1992 presents a truly unique situation: both sides of this equation will almost inexorably undergo a simultaneous in-depth exploration. The primary stimulus for macroanalyses of the Caribbean's history is the Columbian quincentennial—an event that has generated considerable passion regarding the nature and consequences of this encounter between Europe and the Americas. Because the West Indies are where the European intrusion first occurred and where the colonial system persisted the longest, they inevitably find themselves at the epicenter of such controversy.

The Caribbean must now confront the emergence of the new global order. The disintegration of the Soviet bloc, the passing of Cold War bipolarity, the implementation of the Europe 1992 plan, and the growing momentum toward a North American Free Trade regime all lead to a radically restructured international environment wherein small countries such as those in the CARICOM region face the daunting prospect of acclimating to radically new (and potentially disadvantageous) rules of the international game. In short, 1992 is a crucial juncture in West Indian life when, like it or not, serious soul-searching is unavoidable.

The fact that this book coincides with and addresses some of the key issues in what may be one of the Caribbean's watersheds is purely fortuitous, since its conceptual roots can be traced to the mid-1980s. At that time my research agenda was leading me (quite gingerly, it must be admitted) into two areas where I felt there were serious gaps in our thinking: The first involved dependency theory. While much had been written on the nature of dependency and the intricate dynamics that could lead countries into such a quandary, very little was being said about the prospects and processes of moving beyond it. The second gap involved South-South relations, with most of the material focusing on Third World ties to one or both of the superpower metropoles. Virtually no serious attention was being devoted to relations between the developing nations themselves. Obviously these two subjects are extremely complex and merit extensive individual scrutiny. But it likewise became apparent that there may well be areas of important interface between them. This book results from my attempt to probe some of those linkages at both the theoretical and policy analysis levels.

The rationale for choosing the CARICOM experience to serve as my case study was basically twofold. First, since dependency theory has to a great extent been developed within the sphere of Latin American–Caribbean studies, it seems appropriate that initial forays into postdependency theory utilize the same venue. Second, the vulnerabilities of small island societies such as in the West Indies provide a powerful incentive for them to find ways to augment their influence as they move out onto the international stage where they will inevitably have to confront much stronger actors. The CARICOM states have traditionally displayed considerable interest in utilizing a South-South strategy to achieve this end, the classical example being their participation and leadership within the Lomé process. Thus, they emerge as excellent candidates for a case study in the problems and prospects of small-state postdependency South-South politics. I hope that other, similar investigations along these lines will follow. I have, for example, attempted to incorporate various concepts developed here into some of my analyses of Cuba's foreign relations.[1]

Some might contend that the reverses suffered by proponents of Marxism in the USSR and elsewhere, combined with the restructuring of the international system flowing from the collapse of the Soviet bloc, have engendered an environment that makes the issues being raised here essentially immaterial. Specifically, there are those who insist that the disarray afflicting the radical left in many parts of the world has totally discredited its ideology and proved that its ideas—including dependency theory—are totally inappropriate to contemporary realities. Others reach similar conclusions about the whole concept of the Third World, arguing that the only significant factor imparting any real sense of unity or purpose to this loose amalgam of disparate states was the bipolar competition that until recently dominated foreign affairs. In other words, according to this perspective, South-South relations could be seen as having any serious theoretical or practical significance only within the context of the exigencies and opportunities created by the Cold War. Thus, the demise of superpower bipolarity likewise comes to be seen as the death knell of the South-South dimension as an important component of the global scene.

When subjected to scrutiny, however, such assertions are not persuasive. Radical dependency theory, for instance, never relied on the existence of a socialist order in the USSR or elsewhere for its cogency. To the contrary, it always emphasized that a capitalist world order dominated by a limited number of great powers is exactly the kind of situation wherein less-developed countries (LDCs) are most likely to find themselves locked into the status of peripheral, dependent states. To the extent that the situation emerging from the ashes of the Cold War is configured along the lines of this classic western model, the whole dependency-postdependency issue is likely to become an increasingly important and contentious element of the North-South dialog. Though the demise of the socialist camp (i.e., the Second World) might render the notion of a Third World irrelevant in an abstract conceptual sense, in practice the LDCs are going to have to find an alternative counterweight to the power and influence of the industrialized West. Certainly one alternative is to achieve much higher levels of policy coordination and bargaining unity, which in essence means that the brave new dawn of postbipolarity may give added impetus to South-South relations rather than rendering them irrelevant.

While this book clearly does not involve a cast of thousands in the epic cinematic sense, it was indeed years in the making, during which some significant debts of gratitude were incurred. Unfortunately, a mere expression of thanks never adequately conveys its recipient's immense contribution. Recognizing, then, that much more is owed than is being given, I express my appreciation to Janice Byrd of the Council for the International Exchange of Scholars, who helped to arrange a Senior Fulbright Fellowship that allowed me to undertake nine months of field research and teaching in the Caribbean; to Anthony Bryan and his colleagues in the Institute of International Relations at the University of the West Indies (St. Augustine, Trinidad), who served as my hosts and mentors as well as becoming my good friends during my Fulbright sojourn; to Lynne Rienner of Lynne Rienner Publishers, whose patience with my delays in completing the manuscript and whose support despite my transgressions went far beyond the call of duty; to Laura Wilburn (administrative secretary) and Jennifer Brown (student assistant) of the Political Science Department at Indiana State University, whose logistical assistance and especially expertise in computerized word processing were invaluable in preparing the manuscript; and, saving the most important until last, to my wife, Marge, and my daughter, Tamara, who have allowed me to continue to live in relative tranquillity despite the fact that their own lives were often totally disrupted by my work.

H. Michael Erisman
April 1992

Note

1. See, e.g., H. Michael Erisman, "Cuba's Foreign Policy: Post-Dependency Impulses and Security Imperatives," *Harvard International Review* 9, no. 2 (January 1987): 33–36; and H. Michael Erisman and John M. Kirk, "Introduction: Cuba and the Struggle for Political Space in the 1990s," in H. Michael Erisman and John M. Kirk, eds., *Cuban Foreign Policy Confronts a New International Order* (Boulder, CO: Lynne Rienner Publishers, 1991), pp. 1–17.

1

The CARICOM States and International Relations: A Macroperspective

To the casual outside observer, the English-speaking Caribbean often appears little more than a hedonistic way station where one pauses in the pursuit of sun-splashed pleasure. But lurking behind the stereotypes nurtured by travel brochures and sanitized images of dashing buccaneers and romantic plantation life is the harsh reality of what West Indian writer V. S. Naipaul calls the "Third World's Third World," a conglomeration of former British colonies known collectively as the CARICOM states, whose ongoing struggle for socioeconomic development is seriously complicated by an unusual and indeed daunting combination of historical and geopolitical factors. Inevitably, the convergence of such multifaceted currents has a major impact on the dynamics of the region's international relations.

The term *CARICOM* refers specifically to the Caribbean Common Market and Community, a regional organization of English-speaking countries formed in 1973 to promote economic integration, cooperation in various functional areas (e.g., health, education, communications, transportation), and foreign policy coordination. CARICOM is a direct descendant of the West Indies Federation and CARIFTA (the Caribbean Free Trade Association). The Federation, an unsuccessful attempt at preindependence political unification, operated from 1958 to 1962. In 1968 its ten former participants, along with Guyana, founded CARIFTA, which subsequently evolved into CARICOM. Currently CARICOM's thirteen members (their dates of independence from Great Britain are given in parentheses) are Jamaica (1962), Trinidad and Tobago (1962), Barbados (1966), Guyana (1966), the Bahamas (1973), Grenada (1974), Dominica (1978), St. Lucia (1979), St. Vincent and the Grenadines (1979), Antigua and Barbuda (1981), Belize (1981), St. Kitts–Nevis (1983), and Montserrat (the only nonindependent territory in the organization).[1]

Two features in particular have profoundly influenced the basic configuration and dynamics of the CARICOM countries' interactions with

1

the outside world and in fact make the area in many respects a unique subsystem within the larger international arena. First, the CARICOM region (and the larger Caribbean Basin)[2] has long been recognized as one of the globe's premier crossroads; through it and into it have flowed goods, people, and cultural influences from Europe, North America, Africa, Latin America, and, to a somewhat lesser extent, the Near and Far East. Second, the CARICOM area constitutes perhaps the largest concentration in the world of small developing nations that are to a fairly significant degree regionally integrated. Historically, the crossroads factor has meant that the Caribbean Basin in general and the CARICOM region in particular have been a cockpit of great power competition. This centuries-old struggle, which has raged from almost the very moment that Columbus first set foot in the New World, initially involved a wild scramble for colonial holdings among France, Spain, and Britain, with the Dutch also participating. Subsequently, however, this European preeminence was gradually but inexorably displaced by the growing strength and influence of the United States—the Colossus of the North.[3]

Although ideological crusading has sometimes (especially on Washington's part) been an element behind such external penetration, economic and strategic considerations have usually been the main motivations. The primary function of the plantation societies the European colonial powers established in the Caribbean was, of course, to generate wealth that would then be transferred to the home country through a variety of mechanisms. In some instances the results were rather spectacular, as evidenced by the fact that England at one time displayed a willingness to trade Canada for the sugar-rich French islands of Martinique and Guadeloupe. The United States, despite being a latecomer to the struggle for Caribbean influence, also quickly developed substantial economic interests there. In fact, even prior to the Revolution,

> the American colonies were an important part in the triangular trade among Britain, the colonies themselves, and the Caribbean. In 1770 the colonies supplied the bulk of the islands' basic foodstuffs and other needs: half of the flour, all of the butter and cheese, one-third of imported dried fish, one-quarter of the rice, all of the lumber, and all of the pasture animals. Indeed the prosperity of New England was due largely to its trade with the West Indies.[4]

The patterns of U.S. economic relations with the West Indies inevitably changed over time, with the overall trend in recent years indicating that the region's relative importance to the United States as a trading partner and a magnet for private investment has declined somewhat. Yet the United States still relies on Jamaica and Guyana to furnish approximately one-third of its foreign bauxite, U.S. multinational corporations continue to be heavily and very profitably involved in the CARICOM region,[5] and close to one-half of all U.S. seaborne exports and imports flow through the Caribbean.

Turning to the strategic side of the equation, even a cursory glance at any maritime map reveals that the many military and commercial sea lanes traversing the Caribbean and the Gulf of Mexico are vulnerable to interdiction at several natural choke points, the most prominent being the Yucatán Channel, the Straits of Florida, and the Windward, Mona, Anegeda, and Galleons passages, as well as, of course, the man-made Panama Canal. Since the territories adjacent to these bottlenecks have almost always been deemed potentially crucial pieces of real estate by naval strategists, first the European colonial powers and then the United States were prone to look on control of the Caribbean archipelago as involving vital national interests.[6]

But regardless of the specific factors that have functioned to make the Caribbean a great power crossroads, the end result has always been the same—the region has become an *object* of foreign domination, and its history has consequently been written to a great extent in terms of its incorporation into various European colonial empires and later into the U.S. sphere of influence. Not surprisingly, this legacy has had a profound impact on current perceptions regarding the basic dynamics of the relationship between the CARICOM states and the outside world, with some observers inclined to approach the topic from a power politics perspective while others prefer to employ a dependency framework.

When the crossroads characteristic is combined with the current reality of the CARICOM area as a unique concentration of small, regionally integrated developing states, the West Indies emerge as an excellent laboratory for exploring the evolving status and role of such countries in contemporary international relations. But perhaps more important, the CARICOM nations, in contrast to most of their counterparts elsewhere, have often managed to achieve a degree of coordination in their foreign policies that in turn confers on the region a distinct and in many respects a special international personality. Specifically, says Paul Sutton, the CARICOM area "has been defined from without as a collective unit at the same time as a collective self-identity has developed from within, the one fortuitously reinforcing the other in respect of the pursuit of tangible interests in the international system. This . . . established a presence for the region in international politics in 1980 which it did not possess in 1970 and which in the future it may be hoped will yield . . . returns so far denied."[7] Such efforts to establish a tradition of foreign policy collaboration represent a concrete example of the fascinating and rather rare phenomenon of small Third World countries attempting to influence the structure and dynamics not only of their regional subsystem, but also the international system as a whole.

Unfortunately, however, such ambitions must confront the problem of size versus viability. The CARICOM countries, whether individually or collectively, are small by international standards. Admittedly, merely because a country is small (measured in terms of physical area, population, or both) does not necessarily mean that it likewise will be weak or somehow severely handicapped, as is graphically demonstrated by the experiences of such nations as Luxembourg, Israel, Norway, and Singapore. In the West Indies, however, one generally finds not just small states, but rather microstates,[8] whose size does tend to involve such inherent liabilities as the lack of a local market capable of supporting a modern, diversified domestic economy; very high per capita costs for public services and the development or maintenance of a solid economic infrastructure; and difficulties in retaining high-quality administrators, managers, scientists, and technicians. Complicating this situation is the fact that most CARICOM states are not particularly well endowed with the type of natural resources that today are normally considered to have a high development potential. The only exceptions are Trinidad and Tobago, which has significant petroleum reserves, and Jamaica and Guyana, which are major bauxite exporters. All three countries, however, suffered serious setbacks during the 1980s as world market prices for these commodities plunged.

Such size and resource problems have resulted in vulnerabilities reflected in the track record of the CARICOM economies. Granted, the picture is not completely bleak. Measured by certain indices, living standards and the quality of life are markedly higher in the West Indies than in many other developing countries. In particular, the figures on literacy rates, life spans, and infant mortality all indicate that the educational and health care services available in CARICOM societies exceed Third World norms. The per capita income figures are also quite respectable in several cases.[9] But move beyond these pockets of high performance and one finds broad patterns of weakness. For instance, over half of the CARICOM nations experienced zero or negative real per capita growth rates during the 1970s,[10] and the situation did not improve in the 1980s. Plagued by drastic price drops in international markets for their commodity exports and growing debts to cover their trade deficits, most CARICOM countries floundered, deep in a crisis of declining productivity aggravated by increasing inflation and chronic unemployment and underemployment rates that often ran as high as 40–50 percent.[11]

Such size-related considerations ultimately raise the question of whether the CARICOM countries really have the capacity to function as truly viable national entities in the modern world. Or will they succumb to what Hans Vogel calls a self-increasing deficit of autonomy as structural scarcities generate a chain reaction of developments that culminate in a high probability for foreign penetration of their economic-political decisionmaking processes?[12] Probably no one has posed the problems resulting from the convergence of historical domination and size-versus-viability factors more eloquently than William Demas, who lamented the fact that

> many people in the region . . . hold pessimistic and deterministic positions regarding our prospects for any degree of *effective* independence vis-a-vis the outside world. They believe that we are doomed to abject subordination because of our small and in some cases minuscule size, and because of our long colonial history as mere political, economic, military, and cultural appendages of the metropolitan countries. They consider that we can only be "specks of dust" . . . impotent, unable to control our destiny, imitative rather than innovative and inevitably subject to the decisions, and indeed the whims, of outside countries, nearly all of whom are much larger and much more powerful than we. In particular, they argue that all the weaknesses just mentioned are intensified because of geopolitical factors (principally our location in the "backyard" of a superpower and our close proximity to much larger and more powerful Third World countries).[13]

To assure that this dreary scenario does not become permanent reality, Demas concludes, West Indian states must dedicate themselves to the arduous, long-term struggle of translating their *formal* sovereignty into *effective* sovereignty (an effort that is be discussed here in terms of postdependency politics). This task, because it clearly entails a close interface between the domestic dynamics of development and a country's international relations, inevitably leads to a heavy focus on both the current and potential future roles of the CARICOM nations in world affairs. But rather than concentrating on such traditional concerns as the relations of the CARICOM nations with the region's dominant metropolitan powers or with each other as they have pursued various integration schemes, I probe an aspect of CARICOM foreign policies that has too often been neglected—the South-South (or Third World) dimension.

The Role of CARICOM States in International Affairs

A state's status and behavior in the global arena can be influenced by such diverse variables as changes in the international system's balance of power, perceived security threats, historical conditioning, its natural attributes, its choice of developmental models, its government's ideological orientation, its decisionmaking mechanisms, and its leaders' personalities.[14] Within this vast array of theories and conceptual frameworks, it is probably fair to say, while admittedly simplifying somewhat, that the role of the CARICOM countries in world affairs has generally been approached from one of three basic macroperspectives: power politics; interdependence/integration; or dependency. Although these paradigms are not mutually exclusive, each does have a particular emphasis that affects not only how the main problems confronting West Indian societies are defined and prioritized, but also what are seen as the available options from which to choose the most appropriate policy response.

The concept of dependency has, of course, become widely utilized to depict the essential nature of the global reality confronting the CARICOM nations. Indeed the emergence of the South-South dimension in the region's external relations can to a significant extent be attributed to growing awareness of and concern about the phenomenon on the part of both government officials and policy influentials in the West Indies. Consequently dependency theory serves here as the analytical starting point for examining the CARICOM countries' evolving Third World ties, the basic goal being to probe the linkages between the South-South axis in their foreign policies and the progression to a postdependency mode of international relations. Among the more specific issues to be addressed are: What is "controlled dependence," and what position does it occupy within the broad spectrum of postdependency politics? Beyond the South-South option, what other strategies of postdependency politics are available? What are the main factors that have facilitated and, on the other hand, impeded CARICOM's South-South pursuit of controlled dependence? And, finally, what are the prospects regarding the future priority CARICOM states may or perhaps should give to the South-South component in their foreign policies? But since the power politics and interdependence/integration perspectives are also relevant to certain aspects of these questions, they require some consideration before turning to an in-depth discussion of dependency and its impact on CARICOM international relations.

Power Politics

The power politics (or realist, as it is also known) school revolves around the notion that the essence of foreign affairs is the constant struggle among states for the power they need in order to be able to pursue and protect their vital egocentric interests, the foremost being national security. Thus the international arena comes to be looked on as akin to a Hobbesian state of nature wherein relationships are almost invariably competitive, the potential for serious violence is high, and preponderant strength is the only reliable guarantor of survival. But since the supposed logic of the system militates against any one actor always having the capacity to dominate everyone else (because an attempt by any state to increase its power significantly constitutes a possible threat to the security of others that will trigger compensatory countermoves), a delicate but nevertheless viable long-term equilibrium is prone to emerge based on a dynamic balance of power.

This realist scenario, which has been embraced by many academics and makers of foreign policy, offers little that is encouraging to smaller states such as the CARICOM countries, for the interests of the weak are routinely sacrificed to the preferences of the strong in a world where power is considered the only unit of political currency that really matters. Indeed, given their propensity for Social Darwinism, most realists do not seem especially concerned by the fact that their rules of the international game almost always lead to a situation wherein the opportunity for individual small countries to control their destinies is minimal (the only notable exceptions occurring in those cases where they are ignored because the major actors deem them so unimportant or where they are able to maintain some independent political space by carefully playing the power centers off against one another). Instead, small states tend to be seen as the inevitable victims of the global hierarchy of nations created by power differentials; their role, as epitomized by the West Indian experience over the centuries, is to be incorporated into a sphere of great power influence. It is, from the realists' viewpoint, immaterial whether the immediate impetus for this subordination comes from a government involved in some form of empire building or from a small nation seeking a protective patron, for in either instance the outcome can ultimately be attributed to the harsh and inexorable exigencies of power politics.

While it might be argued that the realist perspective can provide some insights into the historical dynamics that led the West Indies into dependency, the same cannot be said with regard to its utility as a conceptual framework for generating guidelines to help alleviate the problem. The roots of this inability can be traced to the theory's great power bias, which, for example, prompted its proponents during the Cold War era to view the Caribbean as simply another theater in the U.S.–Soviet struggle for global influence. As such, the South-South and even the North-South dimensions of CARICOM international relations, where dependency is more likely to emerge as a major concern, tend to be ignored. This is consistent with the realists' propensity to make a clear distinction between what they consider "high politics" (involving military-security issues with significant implications for the global power balance) and "low politics" (entailing internationally linked aspects of socioeconomic development), with the former generally being seen as dominating or structuring the overall environment in which the latter operates. Since Third World dependency and related questions fall into the second category, they represent low-priority items in the realist approach to international relations in the West Indies and elsewhere. Thus, to the extent that power politics serves as the main foreign policy paradigm for CARICOM leaders, the prospects for serious progress in pursuing counterdependency initiatives are not promising.

Interdependence/Integration

Compared to the realist and dependency schools, the interdependence/ integration perspective is often much less pessimistic about the structural asymmetries that exist at the international level and their negative implications for small Third World states. This is not to say that the dangers inherent in the inevitable power discrepancies within the global community are naively ignored, but rather that emphasis tends to be placed on the positive aspects of the pervasive patterns of interdependence that characterize the modern world, with integration seen as an effective mechanism for transforming the potential for benefits into reality.

The contemporary world has, to use a popular cliché, definitely become smaller in the sense that the emergence of a more coherent international economy, combined with startling advances in communications and transportation technology, means that a highly complex web of global interactions has developed that reaches into almost every corner of the earth. Thus, to paraphrase John Donne, practically no country today can be an island, entire of itself; each is to some degree a piece of the economic continent, a part of the sociocultural main. It is upon this basic reality that the concept of interdependence rests.

Technically, interdependence can be defined as a condition wherein "events occurring in any given part or within any given component unit of a world system affect (either physically or perceptually) events taking place in each of the other parts or component units of the system."[15] Depending, of course, on the type of system involved, interdependence can assume various functional forms as well as operate at different levels of analysis (e.g., global, regional, bilateral).

As summarized above, interdependence[16] refers essentially to relationships entailing *sensitivities,* which simply means that the component parties will be mutually (though not necessarily equally) responsive to changes that occur within the overall framework of their association. Moreover, those who are prone to be more upbeat view these sensitivities in a favorable light, emphasizing that they usually produce benefits for everyone involved that outweigh the costs. In other words, what is supposedly transpiring is a positive-sum game in which all the actors profit, although admittedly power or other differentials frequently cause the rewards to be distributed unevenly. But despite any flaws, interdependence is basically seen as a benign phenomenon and thus is to be applauded and promoted rather than condemned. Indeed, according to this viewpoint, the main thrust of international politics should not be to reduce interdependency, but instead to manage it effectively and thereby improve the overall quality of life within the world community.

Realistically, however, it is recognized that interdependence can also generate *vulnerabilities,* which refers to a situation wherein a country is highly likely to be adversely affected by modifications within the general structure of its external ties. In these instances, which are most common when states such as those in the CARICOM region (whose small size raises questions about viability) are dealing with larger, more developed nations, interdependence can take the form of a zero-sum game where all the significant benefits are monopolized by a few powerful players. Since such asymmetrical relationships cannot always be avoided, it becomes imperative to find mechanisms for minimizing the potential liabilities. One possible alternative is regional integration.[17]

Regional integration normally involves a number of countries coordinating their policies and pooling their resources in order to achieve as a group higher levels of socioeconomic development than would be possible if they continued to operate individually. Theoretically, this process of economic integration/modernization will be facilitated and accelerated if it is accompanied by a certain degree of political unification whereby participating states delegate the authority to make some choices regarding the allocation of values and resources to collective decisionmaking bodies functioning at the regional level. In practice, however, governments have usually been extremely reluctant to abdicate any of their traditional sovereign prerogatives, opting instead for the more palatable option of policy coordination. In any case, regional integration does provide a possible means for small countries to address the size-versus-viability problem and to increase their performance capabilities at the international level, thereby positioning themselves to take advantage of whatever opportunities interdependence presents.

Much more so than the realist school, the interdependence/integration perspective provides a conceptual framework for gaining an appreciation of the primary issues and problems that tend to dominate the international agendas of West Indian governments, especially with regard to their North-South relations (where vulnerability rooted in asymmetrical interdependence is highly relevant) and to their emerging patterns of South-South cooperation (the most firmly established being the CARICOM experiment in regional integration).[18] Yet these admitted assets are not sufficient to overcome the qualms of those who feel that the approach's optimism about the potential benefits of interdependence is grossly unwarranted and hardly justified by Caribbean realities. Foremost among these critics are, of course, the dependency theorists.

Dependency Theory

The intellectual roots of dependency theory, which attributes the underdevelopment of Third World states primarily to external factors that have relegated them to an inferior and often exploited status in the international community, can be traced to three fundamental sources: classical Marxist writings on imperialism, especially by Lenin and his disciples; the promulgation in the postcolonial period, mainly by Third World scholars, of such concepts as neocolonialism and neoimperialism; and the early work of various Latin American economists associated with the United Nations Economic Commission for Latin America (ECLA).[19] The last group, often called the Prebisch school (after its leading exponent, Raúl Prebisch), was initially the most influential in refining Latin American dependency theory. Its scope of inquiry, however, has been somewhat narrow, concentrating mainly on the negative developmental implications arising from the unequal terms of trade between the northern industrialized societies and the less developed countries (LDCs). The Third World nations cannot, according to this view, ever expect to significantly improve their relative position in the global economic arena as long as they remain locked into trade relationships whereby they mostly export a few low-priced commodities to the industrialized states while simultaneously importing expensive manufactured products from them. Defining dependency basically as the uneven development inherent in, and promoted by, these economic imbalances, ECLA analysts have sought remedies in such strategies as diversifying Third World exports, import substitution (i.e., establishing domestic companies to service local consumer markets instead of relying on imports to do so), and regional integration. In short, they are inclined to perceive dependency as a technical problem rather than the product of fundamental flaws within the capitalist structure of the international economic system. Consequently, the solutions they espouse have essentially represented reforms geared toward more state involvement in internal capitalistic development and heavier emphasis on economic nationalism (as opposed to free trade) in the relations of the LDCs with the industrialized world.

Eventually, the Prebisch school's basically moderate perspective was overshadowed by a more radical approach that went beyond the purely economic ties involved in dependency and began to explore the phenomenon in terms of the sociopolitical dynamics operative within the LDCs and the developed nations and also at the level of their international linkages. In other words, this more comprehensive analysis views dependency as an inherent component of the global economy's capitalistic structure. Moreover, many radical *dependentistas,* believing that this situation was deliberately created and is maintained by the industrialized countries to facilitate their systematic pillaging of the Third World, are quite skeptical and even contemptuous of solutions limited to economic reforms, insisting instead that the real heart of the issue is to be found in the broader configurations of power at both the national and global levels.

From these beginnings, an extensive and complex body of thought evolved. Indeed, although Latin American studies continue to function as its nerve center (with the radical outlook being more vigorous and visible than its ECLA counterpart), dependency theory has become recognized as a major subfield within the larger discipline of international relations.[20] This explosive growth has, however, made it increasingly difficult to succinctly define or summarize dependency theory, for there are subtle yet significant differences in perspective as one shifts from one analytical current to another within the overall mainstream. Ronald Chilcote probably does as good a job as anyone, particularly in highlighting the interface involved between developmental economics and international relations, when he says that

> dependency theory focuses on the problem of foreign penetration in the political economies of Latin America. Generally, this theory explains underdevelopment throughout Latin America as a consequence of outside economic and political influence. More specifically, the economy of certain nations is believed to be conditioned by the relationship of another economy which is dominant and capable of expanding and developing. Thus the interdependence of such economies assumes contrasting forms of dominance and dependence so that dependent nations might develop as a reflection of the expansion of dominant nations or underdevelop as a consequence of their subjective relationship.[21]

While willing to accept the broad outlines of Chilcote's formulation, radical Latin dependentistas would prefer to see greater stress on their contention that the "dominant nations" to which he refers are invariably the highly industrialized capitalist countries, especially the United States. They are therefore committed to a somewhat more specific (and ideologically partisan) conceptualization that views dependency as

> the process of incorporation of less developed countries (LDCs) into the global capitalist system and the "structural distortions" resulting therefrom. . . . This approach proceeds from a structuralist paradigm which focuses on the class structure in the peripheral country, the alliance between this class structure and international capital, and the role of the state in shaping and managing the national, foreign, and class forces that propel development within countries.[22]

Although I recognize that generally this radical viewpoint is indeed the most accurate portrayal of dependency's harsh realities within the Latin American–Caribbean context, the term will nevertheless be used here in a somewhat broader sense to refer to a phenomenon entailing external penetration of a Third World country's economic, political, and/or sociocultural processes that is so pervasive that ultimately crucial decisionmaking power is acquired and exercised by outsiders. The result is that the developing nation *loses control* over certain, and often important, aspects of its domestic and foreign policies. This emphasis on loss of control, which William Demas labels in the case of the CARICOM states a lack of "effective sovereignty," is one of the major elements in the dependency paradigm that distinguishes it from interdependence.

Focusing on these shifts in power is the key to understanding the patterns of exploitation that, according to the dependentistas, are the main characteristic of current North-South relations. The fundamental dynamic involved, they say, is nothing particularly new—power is wielded in the interests of those who have successfully competed to possess it. Although not always openly acknowledged, such selfishly motivated behavior has long been accepted in capitalist societies, the pragmatic rationale being that it is an inevitable outgrowth of the egocentrism that is an ingrained trait of human nature and serves (despite its potential liabilities) as a driving force behind individual and social progress. But when applied within the context of contemporary international power configurations, these rules of the game mean that it is the metropolitan centers (i.e., the industrialized capitalist states) who benefit at the expense of the southern periphery, where underdevelopment is perpetuated as the Third World's human and natural resources (as well as its other forms of wealth) are exploited to underwrite both the North's current high standards of living and its prospects for future growth. Basically, then, dependency emerges as the modern manifestation of classical colonialism. Granted, the specific mechanisms of penetration and control have changed, but the essence of the imperial relationship remains unaltered and can perhaps be most simply described in terms of an informal empire in the sense that "the weaker country is not ruled on a day-to-day basis by resident administrators or increasingly populated by emigrants from the advanced country, but it is nevertheless an empire. The poorer and weaker nation makes its choices within limits set, either directly or indirectly, by the more powerful society and often does so by choosing between alternatives actually formulated by the outsider."[23] In any case, insist the radical dependentistas, the continuing subordination and exploitation of Third World states is neither fortuitous nor random, but rather is integral to the current international economic-political order that is dominated by the highly developed capitalist nations.

The dichotomy between the dominant centers and the subordinate, peripheral countries is not, however, so stark and purely confrontational as it may appear at first glance. In fact, say the radicals, a central feature of dependency's class dynamics is the development of a cooperative, symbiotic relationship between some metropolitan and Third World elites. While both parties will actively seek such an arrangement, the main initiative is usually seen as coming from elements of the LDC's national bourgeoisie (often called the comprador class) who are willing to serve as local agents for, or junior partners of, foreign capitalist interests in order to be assured an ongoing piece of the action. This usually means that the structural patterns of often extreme socioeconomic maldistribution in Third World countries (from which these indigenous elites greatly benefit) are preserved and even intensified. In short, this alliance is based on a convergence of exploitative class interests that subjects the masses in an LDC to a complex pattern of developmental deprecation involving both internal and external dimensions. From the radical perspective, the role played by the Third World clientele bourgeoisie cannot be overemphasized; not only do these elements provide major assistance in facilitating exogenous penetration, but they also help to reinforce and protect the instruments of foreign domination. In other words, driven by their desire for self-aggrandizement, they function as enthusiastic promoters and defenders of dependency.

Latin American dependentistas are especially prone to pinpoint U.S. multinational corporations (MNCs) as frequently providing the linkage between metropolitan centers of economic power and the comprador class in the periphery. Like most foreign investors, these MNCs initially gravitated to such well-established pursuits as mineral extraction or the production of agricultural exports. Later, particularly from the 1950s onward, they began to concentrate on manufacturing as hemispheric experiments with import substitution and regional integration models of development provided them with new opportunities to infiltrate the main arteries of Latin American business and commerce. Also, reflecting what some have called the growing "bankification" of the international economy, large U.S. financial institutions such as Citicorp, Manufacturers Hanover Trust, Chase Manhattan, and Bank of America became increasingly active in the Western Hemisphere, as illustrated by the massive loan portfolios that many of them have put together. Admittedly, a lot of these projects went sour as it became apparent that the debts would probably never be fully liquidated, yet the profit margins were generally quite high on the repayments that have been made, and the banks have to some extent been able to turn to debt-for-equity swaps and other innovative schemes in order to cut their potential losses.[24] These periodic redeployments are, of course, simply indicative of the fact that U.S. multinationals have always focused their attention on the most dynamic sectors of the Latin American economies, moving in quickly and using their already large capabilities to carve out a prominent position on whatever has constituted the "commanding economic heights" at any particular time. In short, MNCs have frequently proved to be very effective vehicles of economic penetration or domination.

Too often there is a tendency, especially on the part of those who have not probed the subject deeply enough, to treat dependency almost exclusively as an economic phenomenon. Such an approach does not, however, sufficiently take into account the fact that there almost inevitably is a considerable interface between any society's economic, political, and cultural subsystems, which means that developments in any one category can have a billiard ball effect leading to modifications in the others.[25] Dependency's long-term growth can be seen as an incremental process composed of various phases that can be defined in terms of the changing or expanding relationships between these subsectors. Basically, what can transpire is that a country initially succumbs to dependency in one issue-area, and then the subsystem interface facilitates a spillover effect that generates dependency in other realms as well. David Lowenthal, discussing cultural neocolonialism in the CARICOM region, indicates that this is exactly what has occurred there. "New forms of dependency reinforce old colonial habits. Political, economic, and cultural constraints are intimately interlinked—commercial ties lead to strategic accommodations, cultural dependency stems from overseas economic dominance. Submission to external cultural criteria is the inevitable concomitant of West Indian political and economic dependence."[26] When a nation reaches the point described by Lowenthal, where its three major societal subsystems—the economic, the political, and the cultural—are all dominated by a foreign metropole, it has fallen into a position of comprehensive dependency; it does not possess effective sovereignty and instead has been incorporated into an informal empire. The evolution of this condition can, for simplicity's sake, be divided into two fundamental stages.

In the first phase economic dependency is initially the most salient feature of the core-periphery relationship. Its roots can vary; it may be the residue of a colonial experience or the outgrowth of becoming locked into unequal patterns of trade, allowing unrestricted private investment from abroad, accepting aid with strings attached from other governments, or running up a large foreign debt. But whatever the specific causes, the end result is external control of a country's economy. Once such subservience is well established, political power—defined here as the capacity to determine the allocation of vital resources and values in a society—has also clearly changed hands, since the responsibility for making macroeconomic developmental decisions, which is normally considered to be the prerogative of a country's government, is now to a great extent being exercised by outsiders. In other words, political dependency has evolved as the natural corollary to economic dependency. The industrialized center, of course, materially benefits from this state of affairs and hence will not hesitate to extend aid to anyone who is willing to help perpetuate it, the primary recipients being those elements of the comprador class and their domestic allies who actually constitute or at least aspire to be the ruling elite in the dependent nation. Under certain conditions the metropole may assume a much more direct role in deciding exactly who will govern, by resorting to covert operations or even open military intervention in order to topple recalcitrant regimes or to prevent radical nationalists from seizing power.

In any case, as illustrated by Figure 1.1, economic and political dependency are at this point well entrenched and mutually reinforcing, thereby creating an environment favorable to the long-term development of cultural dependency.

Figure 1.1 Economic Dependency Triad

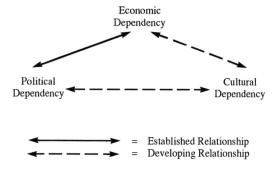

The second phase is characterized by the movement of the cultural component to the forefront of the dependency equation as the center's norms and values, the ideology underlying its organizational structures, and indeed its entire life-style become widely accepted in the periphery as the model to be faithfully emulated. This occurs because the dependent state's socialization processes have been extensively penetrated, and thus its citizens, who have been drawn into the metropole's frame of social reference, have little or no desire to maintain a distinct national identity, preferring, for example, to "live like Americans" or to become "westernized." Consequently, foreign influences now dominate not only the periphery's economic and political systems, but also the hearts and minds of its people.[27]

Theoretically, the periphery's inhabitants will not make significant we/they distinctions when cultural dependency has fully matured, which means that it is potentially the most powerful type: such acculturated individuals would not be likely to realize that cultural dependency (or, for that matter, the economic and political varieties) even exists and therefore would not be inclined to want to alter the status quo. Thus it becomes the keystone holding the comprehensive dependency triad together (see Figure 1.2).

Presented in its most depressing terms, radical dependency theory projects a doomsday scenario wherein, at least for the foreseeable future, the best that Third World countries can hope for is to continue to stagnate at their

Figure 1.2 Comprehensive Dependency Triad

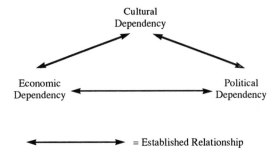

current levels of underdevelopment within the existing capitalist international system. At worst they will sink even deeper into a quagmire of poverty and misery as the prospects become increasingly remote that a new international economic order (NIEO), socialist revolutions, or other significant antidependency initiatives will materialize. Some dependentistas, however, have attempted to make provisions within their paradigms for exceptions to the rule of stark center-periphery dichotomies by introducing the notion of "dependent development,"[28] which revolves around the idea that under certain circumstances an LDC may experience a degree of industrialization and other forms of modernization within the context of a dependency relationship that allows it to rise well above Third World norms. This process is usually thought to be most probable in developing states that satisfy the following two basic prerequisites: (1) they have governments that are willing to become an enthusiastic partner in vigorously promoting indigenous capitalist development; and (2) they enjoy exceptional comparative advantages (e.g., relatively low wage rates given the quality of their labor force) in supplying finished goods consumed in the core countries, or they have a domestic market dynamic enough to support a program of import substitution. It is to such nations, sometimes called newly industrializing countries (NICs), that the large multinational corporations will supposedly be inclined to redeploy their manufacturing operations. But recognize, say the dependentistas, that all this activity is occurring within the overall context of an ongoing dependency relationship; economic progress in the periphery is still to a great extent conditioned by its linkages with the center, and the primary beneficiaries are metropolitan interests along with their comprador allies. In other words, while the productive capacity (especially in the industrial and other modern sectors) of the developing country increases to the point where it can now be considered an NIC rather than a classically underdeveloped Third World state, the basic contours of power within the core-periphery relationship have not been fundamentally altered and hence dependency persists. Proponents of "world systems analysis,"[29] which has been heavily influenced by, and yet is distinct from, the dependency school, have incorporated the NIC phenomenon into their perspective through the concept of the semiperiphery, which is defined as the somewhat economically diversified intermediate level in the international capitalist system's tripartate hierarchy of states where production and other related endeavors are in some instances associated with the highly developed core and in others with the underdeveloped periphery. Operating within this three-tiered framework, these observers emphasize, more than the dependentistas, that regions or individual nations can over time move from one status to another, with changes most likely to occur in either direction along the periphery-semiperiphery axis.

Dependency's impact is not, of course, necessarily limited to developmentally related issues. Indeed, contend the radicals, it rather routinely affects the general foreign policy behavior of peripheral nations, leading them in most cases to pursue courses of action in international affairs that closely parallel and strongly support the preferences of the metropolitan centers to which they are linked. Sometimes this situation results from carrot-and-stick tactics employed by the developed countries: dependency is used to provide substantial rewards for the client state when it acquiesces and to threaten it with the specter of serious retribution should it fail to play its designated role. In other instances, such policy imaging could be based on informal bargaining regarding the terms and conditionalities of dependency, which produces a foreign affairs consensus between the core and the periphery. These two scenarios are most likely to occur in what has been called here Stage 1 of the evolution toward comprehensive dependency. But in Stage 2 such crude manipulation or pragmatic horse trading will tend to be replaced by a much deeper and more complex relationship that functions to fundamentally transform values and attitudes in the LDCs (especially among the comprador class and other influential elements) to the point where the identity of core and periphery elite perceptions translates into foreign policies that are often virtually indistinguishable. This phenomenon is summmarized by William Biddle and John Stephens: "The empirical correlation between the foreign policy choices of dependent states and the preferences of the core states is best seen as the result not of bargaining within an asymmetrical power relationship but rather as the result of an historical process of dependency which shaped and formed the views of the policymaking elites in the dependent states to conform to the preferences of decision-making elites in the core nations."[30] Thus Third World states may display such trappings of independence in international affairs as membership in the Movement of Nonaligned Nations while in reality being seriously deficient in effective foreign policy sovereignty.

Given the convergence in the West Indies of such factors as a crossroads location, a legacy of foreign domination, and possible size-versus-viability problems, it should hardly be surprising that dependency theory has been rather important in shaping people's outlooks concerning the status and role of the CARICOM states in international affairs. Explicitly or implicitly, West Indian academics as well as politicians and government officials have often been inclined to conceptualize many of the region's difficulties and much of its future prospects in terms of dependency. However, as has been the case elsewhere, CARICOM dependentistas have not spoken with a unified voice, gravitating instead into schools of thought with their own distinctive dialects based on subtle theoretical nuances.

The initial impetus behind the development and application of dependency theory in the CARICOM region came from academics associated with the University of the West Indies (UWI) who called themselves the New World Group.[31] Like that of other early dependentistas, their work was strongly influenced by Raúl Prebisch and his followers. Probably the best-known efforts along these lines were those undertaken by Trinidadian Lloyd Best and Canadian economist Kari Levitt,[32] who analyzed the long-term development of Caribbean dependency by probing the evolution of the plantation system in the region from its inception in the early seventeenth century through its contemporary manifestations. It is, they say, the classical plantation economy and its modern variants that have functioned as the mechanism for locking the West Indies into a series of dependency relationships with a shifting cast of metropolitan characters (i.e., first the European colonial powers and then the United States). George Beckford, Norman Girvan, and Alister McIntyre are among the other important contributors to the New World branch of the Prebisch school,[33] many of whom later went on to assume high technocratic positions within the CARICOM area or with international developmental organizations. For instance, Girvan became head of Jamaica's National Planning Agency in the 1970s during Michael Manley's administration, McIntyre was appointed deputy secretary-general of UNCTAD (United Nations Conference on Trade and Development), and Courtney Blackman served as governor of Barbados' Central Bank. Meanwhile, in contrast to the ECLA approach, the radical perspective on dependency was slower to take root in the West Indies. Gradually, however, it became rather well entrenched. Its first major exponent was Clive Thomas, a founding member of the New World Group who subsequently broke ranks in order to pursue a more neo-Marxian path of analysis that would ultimately lead him to conclude that a comprehensive socialist model of development is the only viable alternative to continued dependency that is available to the West Indies.[34] Among the radical dependentistas who became prominent as leading left-wing political activists are UWI lecturers Trevor Munroe of the Jamaican Workers' Party and Ralph Gonsalves of St. Vincent's United People's

Movement as well as, of course, Maurice Bishop and the New Jewel Movement in Grenada.

Despite their many analytical and ideological differences, practically all dependentistas in the West Indies and elsewhere agree on one fundamental point: there is in the overwhelming majority of cases a negative correlation between dependency and the long-term developmental prospects of (small) Third World states. It therefore is, to say the least, quite strange that a great deal of concerted attention within the field has not been devoted to exploring, at both the theoretical and practical levels, the intricacies of counterdependency dynamics.

Beyond Dependency: A Brief Overview

In certain technical respects it is not surprising that dependency theorists have not been particularly inclined to look very far beyond their present conceptual parameters (at what some have called the process of dependency reversal). Their field is, after all, still relatively new, and the phenomena with which it deals are extremely complex. Thus it is understandable that most of the work done thus far has concentrated on dependency's growth and development rather than its possible eclipse as a major feature of contemporary international relations. This tendency has, moreover, been enhanced by various substantive factors that have generated among the theory's proponents widespread pessimism regarding the near-term prospects for any significant modifications in the existing global patterns of dependency.

The more radical dependentistas have been most prone to paint themselves into a theoretical corner, for they have made such a powerful case for the emergence and especially the consolidation of dependency as to create the impression that very little can be done to alter the situation short of cataclysmic revolution across a broad spectrum of Third World and perhaps even developed states. Cal Clark aptly summarizes the problem.

> The exploitation and particularly the distortion and retardation of the dependent economy which dependencia theory sees as integral to dependence should result in a widening of the capabilities between the dominant and subordinate states; so that their structural inequality should increase over time. . . . Even when economic concessions are used to augment dependence for political purposes, it would be a rare center of power that would be foolhardy enough not to turn off the spigot long before any significant change occurred in the structural inequalities between the dominant and dependent partners. Thus, under normal conditions dependence should increase the dyadic structural inequalities between the dominant and dependent partners.[35]

In other words, the essential thrust of dependency is toward self-reinforcement rather than the creation of conditions conducive to its diminution, with the comprador class playing a central role in this equation because its interests are served best by perpetuating the periphery's subordination to the core.

Many theorists, however, contend that the global system, like any other, is over the long run much more dynamic than the dependentistas' scenario suggests; alterations in its configuration and in the linkages between its constituent units can occur. Morton Kaplan was one of the first modern international affairs specialists to vigorously pursue this line of reasoning, contending that there can develop within the broad parameters of any system a number of different system states, each representing a distinct pattern with regard to the variables that constitute the overall system and the relationships between them. To present this position accurately, it is necessary to quote rather extensively from Kaplan.

> Scientific politics can develop only if the materials of politics are treated in terms of systems of action. A system of action is a set of variables so related, in contradistinction to its environment, that describable behavioral regularities characterize the internal relationships of the variables to each other and the external relationships of the set of individual variables to combinations of external variables.
>
> Since a system has an identity over time, it is necessary to be able to describe it at various times, that is, to describe its successive states. It is also necessary to be able to locate the variable changes which give rise to different succeeding states.
>
> The "state of a system" designates a description of the variables of a system. The doctor's description of such things as pulse, temperature, and respiration constitutes a partial state description of the physiological system. The political scientist's description of such things as the political machinery, the characteristics of various candidates for office, and the temper of the electorate constitutes a partial state description of a political system.[36]

From this perspective, then, dependency can be seen as a particular system state that characterizes the relationships between a specific set of international actors at a certain time. But this situation is not immutable. Change may be triggered by exogenous or endogenous stimuli, the result being the development of, or movement toward, a new system state.

Combining the idea of a dynamic system with the fact that dependency is almost universally perceived, at least by the subordinate parties, in a highly negative light, theorists as well as practitioners of international relations are almost inevitably led to confront the question of what alternatives to dependency may be available and what processes or strategies may be involved in making the transition. It is often accepted that it might be necessary to progress through several stages or system states before dependency is eliminated. This approach, which obviously operates on a rather long-term, evolutionary outlook and is usually reluctant to commit itself to a specific ideological option, stands in stark contrast to the radical dependentistas' emphasis on the need for counterdependency initiatives to take revolutionary forms geared toward a rapid shift from capitalism to socialism within the LDCs that would shortly thereafter produce complementary structural changes at the international level. But in both instances the ultimate goal is the same—to provide a conceptual framework that will facilitate not only the development of postdependency theory, but also the efforts of Third World states to fundamentally redefine their status and role in the world community.

Although most of the initial postdependency work has been basically exploratory, some interesting ideas and hypotheses have nevertheless emerged, perhaps the best known being the semiperiphery concept advanced by world system analysts. However, as noted previously, serious questions can be raised as to whether semiperipheral status simply represents a less exploitative form of dependency rather than a qualitative move beyond it. Such skepticism is based on the notion that the world system school tends to define structural change on the periphery-semiperiphery axis primarily in terms of the developmental consequences of the linkages between the metropoles and Third World nations, thereby downplaying the power and class relationships involved. As long as these latter elements remain fundamentally unaltered, say the critics, the most one can say is that some superficial modifications in dependency's economic impact have occurred, but the LDCs have made no major progress toward regaining control over their destinies or toward positioning themselves to exercise effective sovereignty. In other words, the semiperiphery does not constitute a new system state, but instead is only a cosmetic reconfiguration of dependency's essential characteristics. Given such possible problems with world system theory, other approaches to conceptualizing postdependency dynamics have attracted attention, the foremost being the strategic dependency scenario, the seeds of destruction hypothesis, and the collective self-reliance perspective.

The strategic dependency scenario begins from the same basic premise as does interdependency analysis; that is, few if any countries today are or can be self-sufficient, but instead must participate in the international economy in order to remain viable. However, rather than concentrating on the potential vulnerabilities that interdependency creates with respect to the LDCs, the strategic dependency approach reverses the equation by focusing on the core nations. Specifically, it is contended that the more highly developed and complex a modern industrial or postindustrial society becomes, the greater its reliance for its continued prosperity and its future growth on access to critical raw materials, cheap labor, and new markets that in many instances are to be found in the Third World. When the situation has reached a point where the rupture or even just the destabilization of such foreign linkages would involve serious costs for the metropole as a whole or important components within it (e.g., the large MNCs based in the leading capitalist states), a situation of strategic dependency has emerged. Indeed, says Heraldo Muñoz, "Following the Hegelian thesis that the master-slave relationship produces a dialectical dependency of the master on the slave, one could postulate that the strategic dependency of the centers on the periphery is an unavoidable consequence of the development of capitalism at the world level."[37] As opposed to the interdependence school, which views the external restraints on the developmental prospects of both core and periphery nations as major incentives for mutually beneficial cooperation, strategic dependency looks on metropole vulnerabilities as opportunities that should be thoroughly and maybe even ruthlessly exploited. In other words, it is argued that strategic dependency represents fulcrums of influence or bargaining power for Third World states that they can and should use to renegotiate the terms of their relations with specific developed countries. Carried out on a broad enough scale, such efforts could conceivably generate considerable momentum toward the ultimate goal of fundamentally restructuring the current international economic order.

There are, however, both theoretical and practical problems that severely restrict this scenario's usefulness, especially when applied to small-state arenas such as the CARICOM region. Conceptually, the term *strategic dependency* is a blatant misnomer, since one is almost never dealing with a situation where a peripheral country has the capability to penetrate and control a core economy or vital sectors thereof. Without this element of domination, dependency in the proper sense cannot exist in strategic or any other form. By creating the erroneous impression that LDCs enjoy the luxury of substantial power when confronting the center, such semantical carelessness seriously obscures the true dynamics and issues in what is actually a bargaining process rather than a dependency relationship. On a much more pragmatic level the opportunities for individual Third World nations to manipulate strategic dependency are likely to be quite limited. Very few developing countries are in a position to regulate the international flow of critical raw materials, and those whose potential domestic market is big enough to confer significant negotiating leverage are also quite limited in number. On the other hand, there is so much cheap labor readily available in the periphery that metropolitan states and their MNCs can easily meet their needs, shifting locales at will and playing one poor LDC off against another. The obvious countermove is to develop collective initiatives in the Third World. But such tactics are, as even an association as successful as OPEC (Organization of Petroleum Exporting Countries) discovered, extremely difficult to implement and especially to sustain over a long period. Thus, on the whole, trying to capitalize on so-called strategic dependency will probably not produce major counterdependency dividends except, of course, when unique or very large nations in the periphery are involved.

The seeds of destruction (SOD) hypothesis revolves around a line of reasoning quite similar to that which led Marx to conclude that capitalism was doomed to dig its own grave. In each case the analysis takes place within a modified Hegelian framework where the laws of dialectical change govern the clash of opposing elements (or contradictions) that exist in all aspects of the material world. Moreover, the common catalyst pinpointed as setting into motion the forces of potential systemic annihilation is the exploitation and deprivations inherent in the prevailing social order. Finally, both perspectives place heavy emphasis on the class dynamics involved in defending and challenging the status quo. The major difference, of course, is the level at which the logic is applied, with Marx operating primarily within the domestic context of advanced capitalist societies, while SOD advocates probe the interface between national and world affairs.

At the heart of the SOD hypothesis is the contention that the frustration and widespread suffering that dependency almost inevitably engenders can unleash a political whirlwind in LDCs that seriously threatens and may eventually shatter the core-comprador alliance that is the keystone holding together the center-periphery relationship. Such challenges, according to Biddle and Stephens, are

> inherent in the system because the very pattern of dependent development itself generates domestic opposition to the development model. In the Latin American and Caribbean regions, this development path has produced sporadic or uneven economic growth, inequitable distributions of income, foreign domination of certain sectors of the economy, and authoritarian political structures. These contradictory characteristics spawn oppositional social movements which challenge the existing political regimes.[38]

Even when these movements do not succeed in gaining formal power and then moving decisively to establish their country's effective sovereignty, this presence may nevertheless promote some fundamental changes in the attitudes of various elites (e.g., government technocrats or the military) that lead these groups to adopt strong antidependency postures or at least become much more sensitive to the concerns of those who oppose rather than support the dependent status quo. For example, in order to strengthen their mass base and perhaps to provide a dramatic symbolic response to popular demands for quick material progress, state authorities may be inclined to turn to policies, such as nationalization, that run counter to the preferences of indigenous and external capitalists. Indeed it is even conceivable that, under certain circumstances, important elements of the bourgeoisie in a Third World nation may conclude that it would be prudent and even beneficial for them to join other social forces in a drive against not only the presence and influence of foreign economic interests, but also the entire structure of dependency.

Admittedly, many radical dependentistas are extremely reluctant to believe that established elites in developing countries might participate in any serious antidependency offensives, since major erosion in the core-periphery linkage would undermine the very foundation upon which their dominant status rests. There are, say the radicals, many quirks and foibles to which those in the comprador class are susceptible, but socioeconomic suicide is definitely not one of them. Yet the dialectic of movement from one system state to another, which the SOD hypothesis is addressing, does not necessarily demand an immediate, total negation of the prior reality. Such revolutionary transformations can, of course, sometimes occur, and when they do, what emerges is not simply a new system state, but rather a whole new system. History, however, indicates that such upheavals, no matter how desirable and even necessary they may be, are extremely rare. Instead, sociopolitical change is usually more cautious and incremental, as in the case where crass pragmatism, based on the principle that it is better to preserve some prerogatives through accommodation than to risk everything in a confrontation, is the main factor motivating bourgeois elements to support campaigns against dependency. At other times Third World elites may succumb to the lure of nationalism and therefore be willing to see the core-periphery relationship altered even though doing so might endanger some of the power and privileges that they previously enjoyed. But whatever the specific situation, the bottom line is that the SOD phenomenon has the potential to function as a crucial causal variable in the postdependency process.

Unlike the strategic dependency scenario and the SOD hypothesis, the self-reliance perspective does not focus primarily on correlations that might exist between a particular configuration of system state variables and the emergence of conditions and attitudes conducive to counterdependency initiatives. Instead, it is mainly concerned with clarifying the postdependency goals of Third World nations and developing an effective strategy for achieving them. In other words, the emphasis is on policy-oriented end-means analysis rather than cause-effect theorizing.

Too often, the proponents of self-reliance assert, underdevelopment is erroneously equated with structural scarcities in human or natural resources. The real problem, they say, is not overall lack of these developmental prerequisites, but rather the fact that they have been drained away, misdirected, and underutilized by the "beggar your neighbor" behavior of the metropolitan centers and their comprador accomplices. The fundamental idea behind self-reliance is thus actually quite simple: more balanced growth, which will better serve to satisfy the basic socioeconomic needs of the Third World masses, demands that the autonomous capabilities of the LDCs to formulate and implement modernization plans need to be greatly enhanced, which in turn implies that the existing inequitable patterns of core-periphery relations will have to be eradicated or at least substantially weakened. Beyond the obvious power considerations involved, there is also a subtle psychological dimension to such sovereignty seeking that is geared toward rectifying the deeply ingrained habit of many Third World peoples of allowing their developmental horizons to be limited to the North-South axis and thereby assuming that the key to progress is nurturing a closer core connection within the context of the prevailing international order.[39] Although the effort to acquire such self-reliance, which has sometimes been referred to as a process of "delinking,"[40] is in theory galvanized by the long-term prospect of total autarky, in practice it usually translates into much more modest policies that concentrate on deemphasizing ties with a narrow spectrum of industrialized countries (i.e., the capitalist metropoles) in favor of a diversified network of developmental relationships radiating both vertically (e.g., toward the more modernized nations in the former Soviet bloc) and horizontally (i.e., toward other Third World nations).

Once it has opted to pursue self-reliance, the next choice confronting a Third World country is whether to do so on its own or in concert with others. Generally unilateralism, despite its intrinsic desirability, quickly proves to be unfeasible, since very few individual LDCs are characterized by the raw economic potential or the bargaining power necessary to make this approach work. Certainly each of the CARICOM states, with the possible exception of Trinidad and Tobago should oil prices once again skyrocket, is woefully lacking in both respects. Thus multilateralism or, as it is commonly called, collective self-reliance has become the norm for most developing states seeking a postdependency strategy.

In its most optimistic conceptualization, collective self-reliance emerges as a form of carefully planned economic integration wherein participants are not chosen (as is so often the case) on the basis of such general considerations as geographic proximity, shared cultural and historical backgrounds, or similar needs, but rather as the result of an extremely detailed analysis of the strengths and deficiencies as well as the precise developmental aspirations of different countries in order to determine exactly where the "proper fit" exists that will maximize the ability of all involved to make significant socioeconomic progress operating mainly within the parameters of the self-reliant partnership. The essential idea, in other words, is to capitalize on and to enhance the collective capabilities of Third World states by using the specific natural and human resources of certain countries to overcome the specific deficiencies of others and vice versa, the outcome being a synergism that might involve nations that are widely scattered around the world and are even at markedly different levels of modernization.

In reality, however, rather than orchestrating finely tuned interfaces among a fairly limited number of states designed to produce a base for self-sustained development within the group, primary emphasis has been placed on operationalizing collective self-reliance through two complementary mechanisms. The first entails devoting greater attention to seizing all opportunities, no matter how minor or how disparate, to increase South-South economic relations and collaboration, the goal being to lessen wherever possible the vulnerability of Third World nations to continued penetration and domination by the traditional metropolitan centers. Concurrent with these horizontal initiatives, groups of LDCs may be encouraged to diversify their ties with the modernized North. The second aspect of this more pragmatic approach to collective self-reliance focuses on the creation of broad multilateral vehicles for pooling the bargaining power of peripheral countries in pursuit of a common agenda, thereby putting them in a much stronger position to negotiate more advantageous developmental arrangements with the industrialized nations. The problem for smaller states such as those in the CARICOM region is to determine what priority they want to place on these two policy approaches to promoting collective self-reliance and exactly what role they can or should play in each instance.[41]

Expanding the frontiers of any field of study is inevitably a long and tortuous task, and has only recently begun with respect to looking beyond dependency. As indicated by this brief summary of the main threads in the existing counterdependency literature, an immense amount of theoretical and related work still needs to be done before anyone is in a position to understand with any great degree of sophistication the complex interaction of causal variables that can set into motion the equally complicated dynamics of system state transitions. Certainly the possible pitfalls involved may prove to be formidable, and the level of frustration may become high. Nevertheless, focusing on the CARICOM nations in order to probe the problems and prospects confronting small Third World states that aspire to enter the largely unexplored realm of postdependency politics, and utilizing as a starting point a conceptual and analytical foundation based to a great extent on ideas contained in the seeds of destruction hypothesis and the collective self-reliance perspective, I seek to contribute to that pioneering endeavor along two paths: by developing the concept of "controlled dependence" as the first stage toward which West Indian LDCs can and should aim in their attempts to progress beyond dependency, the ultimate goal being fundamental structural change that will result in a new international order characterized by balanced interdependence; and by examining the potential of South-South relations as a viable strategy for Caribbean governments to use in their quest to move from dependency to controlled dependence or, as some might prefer to say, to greater effective sovereignty.

Notes

1. Seven of the least developed CARICOM members—Antigua and Barbuda, Dominica, Grenada, Montserrat, St. Kitts–Nevis, St. Lucia, and St. Vincent and the Grenadines—formed a parallel group in 1981 known as the Organization of East Caribbean States in order to service their distinctive development needs. Like CARICOM, the Organization of East Caribbean States involves a free trade arrangement, the East Caribbean Common Market.

2. Because the word *Caribbean* means different things to different people, its casual usage can sometimes generate conceptual confusion. In an attempt to remedy this problem, William Demas ("Foreword," in Richard Millet and W. Marvin Will, eds., *The Restless Caribbean: Changing Patterns of International Relations* [New York: Praeger, 1979], pp. vii–x) suggests that geopolitically the Caribbean can be seen in terms of three concentric circles. These are, from the inside outward: the English-speaking Caribbean islands, including the Bahamas; the Caribbean archipelago, which is composed of all the islands plus the mainland extensions of Guyana, Suriname, and French Guiana (Cayenne) in South America along with Belize in Central America; and the Caribbean Basin, which encompasses the countries in the two prior categories as well as the littoral states of South America, all of Central America, and Mexico. CARICOM (which for our purposes will sometimes be referred to by the generic labels *Caribbean* and *West Indies*) basically draws its membership, with the exceptions of Guyana and Belize, from the first circle.

3. For details, see Richard Millet, "Imperialism, Intervention, and Exploitation: The Historical Context of International Relations in the Caribbean," in Millet and Will, *Restless Caribbean*, pp. 3–18.

4. Kenneth I. Boodhoo, "The Economic Dimension of U.S. Caribbean Policy," in H. Michael Erisman, ed., *The Caribbean Challenge: U.S. Policy in a Volatile Region* (Boulder, CO: Westview Press, 1984), p. 73.

5. See Tom Barry, "Plunder in Paradise," *NACLA Report on the Americas* 18, no. 6 (November–December 1984):32–45, for an excellent, data-laden short summary of the activities of multinational corporations in the Caribbean. For a much more detailed, but somewhat dated analysis, see David Kowalewski, *Transnational Corporations and Caribbean Inequalities* (New York: Praeger, 1982). Carl Stone, *Power in the Caribbean Basin: A Comparative Study of Political Economy* (Philadelphia: Institute for the Study of Human Issues, 1986), p. 106, presents data showing that the total outflow of profits as a percentage of total foreign private investment inflows during 1973–1977 ranged from a low of 55 percent in Barbados to a high of 340 percent in Jamaica and Guyana, with Trinidad and Tobago posting a figure of 200 percent. Stone's data are consistent with the claims of many other observers that the profit margins for foreign investors in the Caribbean tend to be quite high and sometimes exorbitant.

6. Although it might be argued that such traditional geopolitical considerations became irrelevant for nuclear superpowers, the Reagan White House repeatedly emphasized that one of the major reasons that forced it to assume a much higher military-economic profile in the Caribbean Basin was the growing threat that Soviet-sponsored subversion there posed to U.S. naval security. Examples of such comments and analysis by administration officials can be found in Ronald Reagan, "Strategic Importance of El Salvador and Central America," U.S. Department of State, Bureau of Public Affairs, Current Policy no. 464 (March 10, 1983); Nestor D. Sánchez, "The Communist Threat," *Foreign Policy* 52 (Fall 1983):43–50; and U.S. Department of

State and U.S. Department of Defense, *The Soviet-Cuban Connection in Central America and the Caribbean* (March 1985), pp. 3–5.

7. Paul Sutton, "Conclusion: Living with Dependency in the Commonwealth Caribbean," in Anthony Payne and Paul Sutton, eds., *Dependency Under Challenge: The Political Economy of the Commonwealth Caribbean* (Dover, NH: Manchester University Press, 1984), p. 287.

8. Elmer Plischke, *Microstates in World Affairs: Policy Problems and Options* (Washington, DC: American Enterprise Institute for Public Policy Research, 1977), p. 18, classifies states according to the following population categories: microstates (A = under 100,000, B = 100,000–300,000); small states (C = 300,000–1 million, D = 1–5 million); medium states (E = 5–25 million, F = 25–50 million); and large states (G = 50–75 million, H = 75–100 million, I = 100–200 million, J = more than 200 million).

Using these criteria, the English-speaking Caribbean and Central American countries group as follows by 1990 population estimate (in thousands) and square miles, respectively:

A.	Montserrat	12.467	39.5
	St. Kitts–Nevis	40.157	103.0
	Antigua	63.726	170.5
	Dominica	84.854	290.0
	Grenada	84.135	133.0
B.	St. Lucia	153.196	238.0
	St. Vincent	112.646	250.0
	Belize	219.737	8,867.0
	Bahamas	246.491	4,404.0
	Barbados	262.688	166.0
C.	Guyana	764.649	83,000.0
D.	Trinidad and Tobago	1,334.639	1,980.0
	Jamaica	2,441.396	4,400.0

The source for the 1990 population figures is *World Factbook 1990, Electronic Version* (Washington, DC: Central Intelligence Agency, 1990).

9. The CARICOM countries reporting the highest 1990 per capita GNP figures (in U.S. dollars) were the Bahamas at $11,036, Trininad and Tobago at $3,183, Barbados at $5,965, and Jamaica at $1,103. The source for this data is *PC Globe 4.0, Electronic Version* (Tempe, AZ: PC Globe Inc., 1990).

10. The average annual real per capita GNP growth rate percentages for 1970–1979 were, for Antigua, –2.6; Bahamas, –4.7; Barbados, 2.1; Belize, 4.1; Dominica, –3.2; Grenada, –1.3; Guyana, 0.0; Jamaica, –3.7; Montserrat, 3.8; St. Kitts, 1.3; St. Lucia, 2.8; St. Vincent, –1.7; and Trinidad, 4.5. See World Bank, *1981 World Bank Atlas* (Washington, DC: World Bank, 1982), p. 20.

11. Among the best sources of the most current information on economic conditions in the CARICOM region are *Latin American Regional Reports: The Caribbean* and *Caribbean Insight,* both of which are published in London.

12. Hans Vogel, "Small States' Efforts in International Relations: Enlarging the Scope," in Otmar Höll, ed., *Small States in Europe and Dependence* (Boulder, CO: Westview Press, 1983), pp. 54–59.

13. William Demas, *Consolidating Our Independence: The Major Challenge for the West Indies* (Distinguished Lecture Series, Institute of International Relations, University of the West Indies, St. Augustine, Republic of Trinidad and Tobago), p. 12

(emphasis in original). See also Trevor M. A. Farrell, "Decolonization in the English-Speaking Caribbean: Myth or Reality?" in Paget Henry and Carl Stone, eds., *The Newer Caribbean: Decolonization, Democracy and Development* (Philadelphia: Institute for the Study of Human Issues, 1983), pp. 3–13.

14. This list is derived from Jennie K. Lincoln, "Introduction to Latin American Foreign Policy: Global and Regional Dimensions," in Elizabeth Ferris and Jennie Lincoln, eds., *Latin American Foreign Policies: Global and Regional Dimensions* (Boulder, CO: Westview Press, 1981), pp. 3–18; Elizabeth G. Ferris, "Toward a Theory for the Comparative Analysis of Latin American Foreign Policy," in ibid., pp. 239–257; and Alberto van Klaveren, "The Analysis of Latin American Foreign Policies: Theoretical Perspectives," in Heraldo Muñoz and Joseph S. Tulchin, eds., *Latin American Nations in World Politics* (Boulder, CO: Westview Press, 1984), pp. 1–21. Among the best-known general surveys of international relations theory are James N. Rosenau, ed., *International Politics and Foreign Policy*, rev. ed. (New York: Free Press, 1969); and James E. Dougherty and Robert L. Pfaltzgraff, Jr., *Contending Theories of International Relations: A Comprehensive Survey*, 2d ed. (New York: Harper and Row, 1981).

15. This definition as well as extensive explanatory material is in Oran R. Young, "Interdependence in World Politics," *International Journal* 24 (1969):726–750.

16. Among the major works dealing with interdependence theory are Lester B. Brown, *World Without Borders: The Interdependence Of Nations* (New York: Foreign Policy Association, Headline Series, 1972); Richard N. Cooper, *The Economics of Interdependence* (New York: McGraw-Hill, 1968); Robert O. Keohane and Joseph S. Nye, Jr., *Power and Interdependence: World Politics in Transition* (Boston: Little, Brown, 1977); Stephen D. Krasner, ed., *International Regimes* (Ithaca, NY: Cornell University Press, 1983); and James N. Rosenau, *The Study of Global Interdependence: Essays on the Transnationalisation of World Affairs* (New York: Nichols, 1980).

17. For an excellent analysis of the interface between interdependence and integration, see Robert O. Keohane and Joseph S. Nye, Jr., "International Interdependence and Integration," in Fred I. Greenstein and Nelson W. Polsby, eds., *Handbook of Political Science* (Reading, MA: Addison-Wesley, 1975), pp. 363–367.

18. Among the books dealing specifically with West Indian integration are William G. Demas, *West Indian Nationhood and Caribbean Integration* (Barbados: CCC Publishing House, 1974); J. S. Mordecai, *The West Indies: The Federal Negotiations* (London: George Allen and Unwin, 1968); Roy Preiswerk, ed., *Regionalism and the Commonwealth Caribbean* (Trinidad: Institute of International Relations, 1969); and H. Brewster and C. Y. Thomas, *The Dynamics of West Indian Economic Integration* (Mona, Jamaica: Institute of Social and Economic Research, 1967).

19. Works representative of, or related to, these three schools are John A. Hobson, *Imperialism: A Study* (Ann Arbor: University of Michigan Press, 1965); Vladimir I. Lenin, "Imperialism: The Highest Stage of Capitalism," in Robert C. Tucker, ed., *The Lenin Anthology* (New York: W. W. Norton, 1975); Kwame Nkrumah, *Neo-Colonialism: The Last Stage of Imperialism* (New York: International Publishing, 1965); and Raúl Prebisch, *Towards a Dynamic Development Policy for Latin America* (New York: United Nations, 1963).

20. Excellent examples or summaries of the Latin American school of dependency studies can be found in Andre Gunder Frank, *Development and Underdevelopment in Latin America* (New York: Monthly Review Press, 1968); Fernando Cardosa and Enzo Faletto, *Dependency and Development in Latin America*

(Berkeley: University of California Press, 1979); Ronald Chilcote and Joel Edelstein, eds., *Latin America: The Struggle with Dependency and Beyond* (New York: John Wiley and Sons, 1974); and Heraldo Muñoz, ed., *From Dependency to Development* (Boulder, CO: Westview Press, 1981).

21. Ronald Chilcote, "Dependency: A Critical Review of the Literature," *Latin American Perspective* 1, no. 1 (1974):4. Another well-known definition of dependency is that of Teotonio dos Santos, in ibid., p. 4, who says that

> by dependence we mean a situation in which the economy of certain countries is conditioned by the development and expansion of another economy to which the former is subjected. The relation of inter-dependence between two or more economies, and between these and world trade, assumes the form of dependence when some countries (the dominant ones) can expand and be self-sustaining, while other countries (the dependent ones) can do this only as a reflection of that expansion, which can have either a positive or negative effect on their immediate development.

22. James A. Caporaso, "Introduction to the Special Issue of *International Organization* on Dependence and Dependency in the Global System," *International Organization* 32, no. 1 (Winter 1978):1–2.

23. William Appleton Williams, *The Tragedy of American Diplomacy* (New York: Dell, 1962), pp. 47–48.

24. An excellent summary of these repayment alternatives is in Richard S. Weinert, "Swapping the Third World Debt," *Foreign Policy* 65 (Winter 1986–1987):85–97 . For more general discussions of the Latin American debt crisis, see Robert A. Pastor, ed., *Latin America's Debt Crisis: Adjusting to the Past or Planning for the Future?* (Boulder, CO: Lynne Rienner Publishers, 1987); Esperanza Durán, ed., *Latin America and the World Recession* (Cambridge: Royal Institute of International Affairs, 1985); or Howard J. Wiarda, *Latin America at the Crossroads: Debt, Development, and the Future* (Boulder, CO: Westview Press, 1987).

25. This material on the development of a comprehensive dependency triad first appeared in H. Michael Erisman, "Tourism and Cultural Dependency in the West Indies," *Annals of Tourism Research* 10 (1983):337–361.

26. David Lowenthal, *West Indian Societies* (New York: Oxford University Press, 1972), pp. 233, 245.

27. Compared to the more orthodox economic-political dependency theory, very little has been written employing a cultural dependency paradigm. A sampling of works related to this latter view includes Herbert L. Shiller, *Mass Communications and the American Empire* (New York: Beacon Press, 1971); Armand Mattelart, *Multinational Corporations and the Control of Culture: The Ideological Apparatuses of Imperialism* (New York: Humanities Press, 1979); Krishna Kumar, *Transnational Enterprises: Their Impact on Third World Societies and Cultures* (Boulder, CO: Westview Press, 1980); Anthony Smith, *The Geopolitics of Information: How Western Culture Dominates the World* (New York: Oxford University Press, 1980); and Robert Arnove, ed., *Philanthropy and Cultural Imperialism: The Foundations at Home and Abroad* (Bloomington: Indiana University Press, 1982).

28. See Fernando Henrique Cardoso, "Associated-Dependent Development: Theoretical and Practical Implications," in Alfred Stepan, ed., *Authoritarian Brazil* (New Haven, CT: Yale University Press, 1973); and Cardoso and Faletto, *Dependency and Development*.

29. The leading theorist in this school is Immanuel Wallerstein, whose major

works on the subject include *The Modern World-System I: Capitalist Agriculture and the Origins of the European World-Economy in the Sixteenth Century* (New York: Academic Press, 1974); *The Modern World-System II: Mercantilism and the Consolidation of the European World-Economy, 1600–1750* (New York: Academic Press, 1980); and *The Capitalist World-Economy* (Cambridge: Cambridge University Press, 1979).

30. William J. Biddle and John D. Stephens, "Dependency and Foreign Policy: Theory and Practice In Jamaica" (paper presented at the October 1986 conference of the Latin American Studies Association, Boston), pp. 2–3. The Biddle-Stephens summary is based primarily on the work of Bruce E. Moon, "The Foreign Policy of the Dependent State," *International Studies Quarterly* 27 (1983):315–340, and "Consensus or Compliance? Foreign Policy Change and External Dependence," *International Organization* 39, no. 2 (1985):297–329. In his 1985 article (p. 306), Moon writes that "the incorporation of a national elite into an internationalized bourgeoisie produces decisionmakers who, owing not only to the economic interests they share with American elites through economic transactions but also to their shared values and perspectives, produce policy virtually indistinguishable from that which would be generated by American elites."

31. This summary of dependency theory's evolution in the West Indies is based on an excellent short piece by Anthony Payne, "Introduction: Dependency Theory and the Commonwealth Caribbean," in Payne and Sutton, *Dependency Under Challenge*, pp. 1–11.

32. See Lloyd Best and Kari Levitt, *Externally Propelled Industrialization and Growth in the Caribbean* (Montreal: Mimeograph Copy, 1969).

33. Examples of their work include George Beckford, *Persistent Poverty: Underdevelopment in Plantation Economies of the Third World* (Oxford, 1972); Norman Girvan, *The Caribbean Bauxite Industry* (Kingston, 1967); and Alister McIntyre, "Caribbean Economic Community: Some Issues of Trade Policy in the West Indies," in Norman Girvan and Owen Jefferson, eds., *Readings in the Political Economy of the Caribbean* (Kingston: New World Group, 1971).

34. Clive Thomas, *Dependence and Transformation: The Economics of the Transition to Socialism* (New York: Monthly Review Press, 1974). Among the best known of his more recent works is *The Rise of the Authoritarian State in Peripheral Societies* (New York: Monthly Review Press, 1984).

35. Cal Clark, "The Process of Dependence and Dependency Reversal" (paper presented at the March 1980 conference of the International Studies Association, Los Angeles), pp. 9–10.

36. Morton A. Kaplan, *Systems and Process in International Politics* (New York: John Wiley and Sons, 1957), p. 4. See also Robert Dubin, *Theory Building* (New York: Free Press, 1969), pp. 147–164, for an excellent explanation of the system state concept. Dubin concludes that there are four basic analytical issues that must be addressed when applying the system state concept: (1) under what conditions will a given system state persist; (2) when does a given system state cease to exist; (3) is there any patterning in the succession among system states and does knowledge of the present state of a system permit a specific prediction about the particular states that will succeed it; and (4) when does a given system state make the system as a whole permeable, thereby rendering the system as a whole vulnerable to being destroyed and replaced by a new system.

37. Heraldo Muñoz, "The Strategic Dependency of the Centers and the Economic Importance of the Latin American Periphery," in Muñoz, *From Dependency to Development*, p. 60. Muñoz (pp. 59–92) presents an excellent summary of the strategic dependency concept that recognizes its practical (though not

necessarily its theoretical) shortcomings. The descriptive summary in this section borrows heavily from Muñoz.

38. Biddle and Stephens, "Dependency and Foreign Policy," p. 3. Other works pursuing similar lines of analysis include Theodore Moran, "Multinational Corporations and Dependency: A Dialogue for Dependentistas and Non-Dependentistas," *International Organization* (Winter 1978); Evelyne H. Stephens and John D. Stephens, *Democratic Socialism in Jamaica: The Political Movement and Social Transformation in Dependent Capitalism* (Princeton, NJ: Princeton University Press, 1986); and Marcos Kaplan, "Commentary on Ianni," in Julio Cotler and Richard R. Fagan, eds., *Latin America and the United States: The Changing Political Realities* (Stanford, CA: Stanford University Press, 1974).

39. Good summaries of the self-reliance perspective can be found in Karl P. Sauvant, "Organizational Infrastructure for Self-Reliance: The Non-Aligned Countries and the Group of 77," in Breda Pavlic et al., eds., *The Challenges of South-South Cooperation* (Boulder, CO: Westview Press, 1983), pp. 33–35; Enrique Oteiza and Francisco Sercovich, "Selected Issues in Collective Self-Reliance," *International Social Science Journal* 27, no. 4 (1976):664–671; and especially Johan Galtung, "The Politics of Self-Reliance," in Muñoz, *From Dependency to Development*, pp. 173–196.

40. An excellent discussion on the concept of delinking can be found in Carlos Díaz-Alejandro, "Delinking North and South," in Albert Fishlow et al., eds., *Rich and Poor Nations in the World Economy* (New York: McGraw-Hill, 1978).

41. For a good introduction to the topic of collective self-reliance in CARICOM affairs, see Kenneth Hall and Byran Blake, "Collective Self-Reliance: The Case of the Caribbean Community (CARICOM)," in Muñoz, *From Dependency to Development*, pp. 197–206.

2

From Dependency to Controlled Dependence: Postdependency Strategies for the CARICOM States

Postdependency politics can, when stripped to its bare essentials, be summarized as a process involving Third World countries' attempts, either individual or collective, to make and consolidate the transition first from dependency to controlled dependence, then to protointerdependence, and ultimately to balanced interdependence. Of this model's basic components, only the last one contains the potential for fundamental structural change (which in practice will almost surely prove to be extremely difficult to realize), while the other two simply represent different system states in the overall configuration of existing North-South relationships.

Sometimes the impetus for movement within this framework might be generated by events occurring beyond the periphery, as in the case of a metropolitan country's entering a period of decline and thereby finding it more difficult to maintain its network of dependencies. Probably the most vivid twentieth-century illustration of this scenario is the post-1945 disintegration of the British empire. Equally dramatic is Spain's earlier transformation from a center of world power to a stagnant, weak nation that was often ridiculed as a boondocks society by other Europeans. In both of these examples, alterations at the core provided opportunities for those on the periphery to begin to acquire and wield a greater degree of authority over their affairs than before; territories that were formerly colonies became independent, and independent countries whose sovereignty had previously been more formal than effective now found themselves in a better posture to challenge the dominance that their metropoles had traditionally enjoyed.

Other observers, taking a much broader perspective, focus on the counterdependency implications of changes in the distribution of strength and influence among the world's major nations. For instance, drawing on Morton Kaplan's work regarding the various forms that a balance of power system can assume,[1] it is noted that the tight bipolarity that characterized the global scene in the years immediately following World War II was

33

eventually replaced by loose bipolarity, and that multipolarity has emerged as the wave of the 1990s. While such adjustments mainly affect relations between the most highly developed states, there also may very well be significant North-South considerations involved; it is suggested that the LDCs are much more favorably positioned to exercise some truly meaningful control over their destinies when multipolarity or loose bipolarity rather than tight bipolarity is the prevailing international norm.[2]

In the final analysis, however, it is highly likely that most of the momentum behind postdependency transitions will be generated inside rather than outside the Third World, with the seeds of destruction phenomenon, reinforced by the lure of collective self-reliance, usually functioning as the primary stimulus. There may, of course, be developments in core nations or at the macrosystemic level that will facilitate the counterdependency process, but their impact can be seriously diluted or even neutralized by the opposition that the most powerful party in a relationship may display toward attempts to restructure it along more equitable lines. Radical left-wing dependentistas will tend to see such attitudes as an inevitable by-product of the exploitative imperatives inherent in capitalism, while more moderate observers will probably focus on the pragmatic political factors involved, arguing that it may be unreasonable to expect a metropolitan government, especially one confronted with periodic free elections, to pursue policies that may be widely perceived by its constituents as detrimental to the high standard of living associated with their country's privileged status in the international community. But despite their differences, both lines of thought point to the conclusion that the key initiatives behind postdependency politics are almost invariably going to have to come from the developing states.

The optimal Third World scenario foresees such counterdependency efforts eventually producing more equitable patterns of interstate relations in which the major concerns of the participating countries will be cumulatively macrobalanced within a context of dynamic asymmetrical interdependence. Looking at the individual components of this admittedly somewhat unwieldy conceptualization, the term *interdependence* is used to refer to North-South linkages that entail not only sensitivities, but also a capacity on the part of all the actors to affect the outcome of at least some important aspects of their interactions. It is, of course, extremely unlikely that such influence will be equal across the board, since, as Robert Keohane and Joseph Nye point out, "interdependent relationships are [almost always] more or less asymmetrical depending on the characteristics of issue-areas and the attitudes and interests of elites, as well as on the aggregate levels of power of the states involved."[3] Integral to this analysis is the idea that the inevitable power differentials will be dynamic or variable, not static. In other words, some nations will enjoy an advantage in certain policy realms or situations and not in others. These shifting (or dynamic) asymmetries should over the long run engender symbiotic North-South relationships characterized to a significant degree by accommodation and cooperation. In short, what should emerge is a classical positive-sum game wherein for each player the rewards gained will outweigh the costs paid. The distribution of these benefits will, however, be affected by disparities in the capacity to influence, which means that some will profit more than their colleagues. Nevertheless, there should be a basic equilibrium in the sense that the specific configuration of these allocations will change over time or as movement occurs from one issue-area to another, the end result being that the relatively meager shares that a country may receive in some instances will be offset by disportionately high payoffs in other cases. For simplicity's sake, this general phenomenon is subsequently referred to as balanced interdependence.

For the Caribbean nations, however, balanced interdependence (or, as it is sometimes perceived in Third World circles, the achievement of a radically new international economic order) is not an immediate concern, for they are only beginning to delve into the complexities of postdependency politics. Consequently it has been and remains necessary for them, as well as for others interested in the process, to develop at the theoretical and analytical levels a sophisticated understanding of the concept of controlled dependence as a system state distinct from dependency, and of the dynamics involved in making the transition. From the practical policymaking side of the equation it is equally important to explore the various strategies for pursuing postdependency politics that are available to the CARICOM states, with special attention being devoted here to the South-South option.

Dependency Versus Dependence:
The Basic Dialectic of Postdependency Politics

While balanced interdependence is the ultimate prize in any counter-dependency struggle, the immediate action will in most cases take place at the synapse between the dependency and dependence stages. Indeed, making and consolidating the transition across these two system states constitutes in a figurative sense the crucial first step in the long march of postdependency politics.

One problem that immediately becomes apparent when we attempt to probe the transformational dynamics involved here is the fact that one major element in the equation—dependence—has not been particularly well developed in the existing literature. In stark contrast to dependency, the efforts to operationalize dependence have been rudimentary at best, a good example being the attempt to depict it as "external reliance." Applied to the realm of international behavior, external reliance, says Alberto van Klaveren, refers to "the common belief that, within an asymmetrical relationship, the economically dominant country can extract favorable foreign-policy decisions from its dependent economic partner, by virtue of the power levers it has at its disposal."[4] This statement reveals little beyond the already well-known axiom that the powerful can usually coerce concessions from the weak. Defined in such terms, dependence hardly represents anything startlingly new or even mildly novel. Instead it simply stands as a somewhat modernized reiteration of observations whose roots can be traced to the writings of Thucydides, the ancient Indian theorist Kautilya, Niccolò Machiavelli, and similar notables. Obviously, then, some serious attention must be devoted to refining and making distinctive the notion of dependence, for otherwise any attempt to explore the initial phase of postdependency politics will flounder on the shoals of conceptual ambiguity as it becomes increasingly evident that it is unclear exactly where the process is or should be heading. In short, a sophisticated transitional analysis demands a sharp picture not only of where a country currently is (i.e., in a state of dependency), but also of where it is going (i.e., toward dependence).

The work done by interdependence analysts, particularly their recognition of the vulnerability problem, is a logical starting point in the effort to develop a more elaborate and useful conceptualization of dependence. While generally tending to accentuate the positive, the interdependency school does point out that extremely asymmetrical relationships characterized by cumulative or across-the-board inequalities can emerge. Under such circumstances many Third World countries are so potentially susceptible to foreign influence and even outright domination that it becomes increasingly difficult to sustain the idea that interdependence is the most appropriate label for such a set of linkages. Instead, a point is inevitably reached where the external vulnerabilities become the overriding consideration and hence produce a condition qualitatively different from conventional interdependence. The main factor, of course, is the issue of control. Interdependence implies, at its best, a paradigm wherein there are mechanisms of mutual oversight to guarantee that an acceptable level of shared benefits results between the parties involved. Ideally, such regulatory authority will be institutionalized within the context of what are often called international regimes, which are organizations that are voluntarily created by interdependent states to formalize the rules and procedures for promoting international cooperation in usually quite specific issue-areas. Perhaps the best examples of such associations are the specialized (functional) agencies that have grown up around the United Nations. But when minimal levels of order and reciprocity are not achieved, interdependence in the normal benign sense of the term no longer prevails, having in many instances been displaced by the harsh reality of heavily skewed asymmetries that raise the specter of serious unidimensional vulnerabilities for those countries on the lower end of the development-power spectrum. However, since such traits are common to the system states of both dependence and dependency, some further clarifications need to be made to establish dependence as a unique stage on the continuum from dependency to balanced interdependence.

Like the dependentistas, those analysts who focus on the phenomenon of dependence are also concerned with the dynamics and consequences of imbalances within the international community. However, whereas dependency concentrates on the likelihood of the subordinate polity in a dyadic configuration losing its autonomy, dependence refers to a situation where all the actors have the ability, though admittedly not in equal proportions, to affect the nature and parameters of their relationship. James Caporaso explains the distinction by describing

> dependency as the absence of actor autonomy and dependence as a highly asymmetric form of interdependence. With respect to the former usage, one frequently hears of dependency as reflecting non-autonomous developmental possibilities (especially in the Latin American literature), as the lack of true independence from foreign or transnational influences, or as the presence of a series of related domestic, external, and transnational characteristics.
>
> However, we often hear the term dependence used in a different way, as an imbalance in the relationship between two actors. In this definition, the opposite of dependence is interdependence—not autonomy. While autonomy rests on the idea of self-control, interdependence rests on the notion of mutual control. While the logical polar extremes of dependency are complete independence from unwanted causal influences . . . and complete external control, the polar extremes of dependence are absolute asymmetric interdependence (A needs nothing from B, while B depends on A for fulfillment of all its needs) and the opposite asymmentry where B needs nothing from A, but supplies all of A's needs.[5]

In short, the key difference between the two system states can be found in the perceived degree of susceptibility to foreign penetration and domination, with dependency clearly involving a loss of decisionmaking power to outsiders that basically precludes any significant exercise of effective sovereignty. The dependence scenario, on the other hand, while not so naive as to think that Third World countries are or can be immune to exogenous pressure, operates within a framework where the levels of vulnerability are not so severe as to be conducive to the acquisition of pervasive economic, political, and/or cultural hegemony by metropolitan powers.

This differentiation between dependency and dependence on the basis of external vulnerabilities can be further refined by turning to James Rosenau's innovative work on the notion of a "penetrated political system," which he defines as

> one in which *nonmembers of a national society participate directly and authoritatively, through actions taken jointly with the society's members, in*

either the allocation of its values or the mobilization of support on behalf of its goals. The political processes of a penetrated system are conceived to be structurally different from both those of an international political system and those of a national political system. In the former, nonmembers indirectly and nonauthoritatively influence the allocation of a society's values and the mobilization of support for its goals through autonomous rather than through joint action. In the latter, nonmembers of a society do not direct action toward it and thus do not contribute in any way to the allocation of its values or the attainment of its goals.[6]

When a nation has been penetrated, then, the role of foreigners is not limited to merely exerting exogenous influence. Instead, they are intimately involved in another society's internal decisionmaking processes, with such participation being accepted, whether willingly or not, by important elements within the target country's elites and sometimes even by its population at large. Rosenau later goes on to note that the extent of such interventions will inevitably vary, being confined in some cases to one issue-area (e.g., economic affairs) while in other instances it will be much more pervasive and thus have a multidimensional effect. Applying this analytical scheme to the dependency/dependence dichotomy, dependency relationships clearly fall within the penetration framework, their severity being determined by the scope of the intrusion. The most rudimentary or, as it was called in the previous chapter, first-phase form of dependency occurs when a metropole's meddling is restricted to a single policy arena. At the other extreme lies comprehensive dependency, which results when all the major subsystems of a developing nation have been penetrated and consequently it assumes the posture of a prototypical (or "pure") peripheral society. Dependence, on the other hand, implies that a Third World country's vulnerability is basically limited to the conventional kinds of pressure normally employed by the more powerful within a context of international asymmetries. Dependent states thus have a much greater chance to exercise significant decisionmaking autonomy than do those who find themselves mired in dependency.

The fact that the opportunity exists for certain LDCs to hold some sway over their destinies does not, however, mean that it has actually been seized. But some nations will do so and thereby can be said to have moved into the realm of "controlled dependence" where the emphasis is on maximizing effective sovereignty and becoming increasingly self-reliant. Viewed from a macroperspective, achieving these goals usually demands that a developing country have, at a minimum, the political space necessary to bring about a diversification of dependence, thus theoretically minimizing its exposure to any single foreign influence-wielder, or, ideally, enough bargaining power to be able to satisfactorily negotiate the terms of its dependence. Finding an effective means to achieve these ends constitutes the essence of the first stage of postdependency politics.

Controlled Dependence:
The Quest for Political Space and Bargaining Power

Those few scholars who have tried to come to grips with the problem of controlling dependence have generally been somewhat circumspect in their approach, advocating in most cases courses of action that are not particularly bold or ambitious. For example, Hans Mouritzen promotes the idea of "defensive acquiescence," arguing that small states must adapt to dependence by making tactical concessions to external pressure in order to preserve certain important core values (or vital national interests) such as maintaining their territorial integrity or their distinctive socioeconomic identity. Not only, he says, will such behavior allow them to exercise some significant influence over their general destinies, but those who become most adept at such bartering should also be able to play a role in deciding exactly what trade-offs will ultimately be made.[7] This scenario is not, of course, geared to providing Third World nations with anything new in the way of rewards or benefits; instead it is essentially a means to protect what they already have. Operating in a similar vein, Ole Elgstrom conceives dependence control primarily in terms of developing preventive strategies to guarantee that LDCs do not retrogress into some form of dependency.[8]

Moving beyond these rather conservative conceptualizations and drawing together a number of analytical threads that have already been discussed, *controlled dependence* is seen here as representing *an intermediate system state between dependency and balanced (dynamic asymmetrical) interdependence wherein a Third World country has the capacity to prevent exogenous penetration of its decisionmaking processes and to reduce its vulnerability to metropolitan power centers to the point where its developmental dynamics are not basically the reflection of a subordinate relationship with the core, but rather are a reflection of a series of formally or informally negotiated relationships on both horizontal (i.e., South-South) and vertical (i.e., North-South) axes.*

Obviously the key to this whole counterdependency phenomenon revolves around developing the wherewithal to prevent penetration and reduce vulnerabilities, a process that involves expanding the available political space through diversification and the assertive use of bargaining power.

Diversification: Creating Political Space

Generating political space through diversification is not a particularly difficult concept to address at the theoretical level, although the actual modalities of implementation can (as will be discussed later) become rather complex. Basically it involves nurturing a multifaceted network of developmental ties rather than simply continuing to exist within a narrow circle dominated by one or more metropolitan powers, the ultimate goal being to push back as far as possible the constraining socioeconomic-political boundaries within which a Third World government must operate. William Demas, referring to the CARICOM states, summarizes the stakes involved. "Our degree of economic and other forms of effective independence is likely to be increased by a much greater geographical diversification of our trade and economic relationships than is now the case. . . . This issue of geographical (and therefore geopolitical) diversification . . . is fundamental. . . . It literally increases our options and degrees of freedom and can greatly reduce our trade and economic dependence."[9] Such a scenario does not, of course, demand the total eradication of the old center-periphery association. Instead, what is more likely to occur is selective delinkage, which means that certain aspects of a developing nation's international transactions that once transpired solely or primarily within the context of a dependency relationship are gradually shifted outside of that framework. When such restructuring assumes vertical (or North-South) dimensions the former client will put increased emphasis on expanding its connections with a broad cross section of industrialized nations. For example, if a Third World country had previously traded almost exclusively with the United States, selective delinkage could be achieved by reorienting its import-export patterns in such a way as to direct a significant piece of the current action to the EC (European Community) nations or Japan. The same general rules apply when functioning on the horizontal South-South plane, the only major difference here being that there will probably be greater opportunities for the restructuring to take the form of experiments in integration. Such collective counterdependency initiatives might also entail the creation by southern countries of jointly sponsored MNCs (such as the Caribbean Multinational Shipping Company, which was established in 1975 by a number of Caribbean Basin governments), research and development institutes, and producer cartels (e.g., OPEC) designed to raise and stabilize the world market prices of the raw materials that constitute the lifeblood of many Third World economies.

It should not be expected, especially when dealing with small nations such as those in the CARICOM region, that diversification will eliminate or even substantially alleviate the sensitivities of southern states to external stimuli. Indeed the very nature of the contemporary international system, with its fairly high degree of functional interdependence, makes it almost inevitable that developing countries are going to be affected by events in the larger global community. What is envisaged, however, is that their vulnerabilities to continued penetration and domination by the traditional metropolitan centers will be diluted by spreading their foreign relations over a relatively broad spectrum, for it has long been recognized at practically all levels of human endeavor that increased isolation translates into greater susceptibility to exogenous control. Indeed it was this axiom that in the past led European and other empire-builders to employ divide-and-conquer tactics with devastating effectiveness. Diversification, then, can be seen as a particular counterisolation strategy available to Third World countries; it is, speaking figuratively, an exercise in playing the field rather than running the risk of dependency inherent in going steady with some powerful industrialized state.

There are, of course, criticisms that can be leveled against diversification. The notion is probably most distasteful to the radical dependentistas, whose conviction that dependency can only be combatted effectively through revolutionary change means that they are likely to look on diversification not as a means to achieve controlled dependence, but rather as nothing more than a cosmetic rearrangement of an already seriously flawed international order. Others, while not as harsh or as ideologically motivated, also express some qualms about potential liabilities. Bengt Sundelius, for instance, contends that

> the price for [multilateralization] is greater interdependence with the international system as a whole. While bilateral relations can be controlled, the diffusion of ties involves broader sensitivity to world-wide developments. Thus, the possibilities for unintentional societal disturbances may be increased. The use of many partners may reduce the risk of being manipulated by other governments but may also increase the overall threat to social and economic stability and prosperity.[10]

Such caveats notwithstanding, diversification remains an integral element, both conceptually and pragmatically, in the dynamics of the transition to controlled dependence, for once implemented it provides to a Third World government a much larger array of foreign policy options. The change might be likened to the difference between playing a traditional harpsichord and a modern electronic synthesizer; both instruments produce music, but the synthesizer has an infinitely wider range. Indeed the most sophisticated versions can almost reproduce the sound of a full orchestra. And just as the synthesizer expands the available artistic space by offering more choices, so also can diversification increase a developing country's political space.

Although perhaps not immediately apparent, the postdependency implications of acquiring greater political space are substantial. Specifically, the Third World government, like the synthesizer player, will now be able to be much more enterprising in configuring (or orchestrating) its foreign relations, since a broader scope of international linkages translates into a greater ability to construct alternative scenarios and thereby lends that government more possibilities in terms of the ultimate course(s) of action it can pursue. This in turn means that the developing country has in effect gained more decisionmaking power, since a main component of one's ability to perform as a decisionmaker is the availability of choice: the larger the number of options, the greater one's opportunity and hence capacity to make decisions. Finally, and in many respects most important, an increase in decisionmaking power suggests more control over one's destiny. Combining all these considerations, it certainly appears that diversification has the potential to trigger a chain reaction that can contribute significantly to enhancing southern self-reliance by facilitating the transformation of formal sovereignty, which is characteristic of a heavily penetrated, dependent political system where the decisionmaking power of the indigenous authorities is more symbolic than real, into effective sovereignty.

Enlarging a developing country's political space is, however, only the initial step in what is essentially a two-phase sequence to controlled dependence. As such, diversification and all its ramifications do not represent ends unto themselves, but rather can be more accurately seen as a set of preconditions that, once satisfied, place a Third World government in an optimal position to proceed to the second and most crucial plateau in this particular stage (or system state) in the postdependency process—the assertive use of bargaining power.

Assertive Bargaining: Maximizing Controlled Dependence

Certainly one of the most significant aspects of diversification, at least from a long-term counterdependency perspective, is the positive impact it can have on the bargaining effectiveness of Third World states. Game theorists and others have, of course, established that the operational dynamics of the negotiating process can become extremely complex.[11] Yet the basic rules remain fairly simple, two important ones being: (1) always put yourself in a posture where others are bidding for your goods, services, or business; and (2) always be willing and able to walk away from a prospective agreement. Considerable maneuvering space is a crucial element in both of these scenarios: serious bidding will probably not occur unless one has already developed a diversified network of contacts, and abandoning a particular deal is not likely to be feasible unless there are substantial opportunities to make alternative arrangements. When, on the other hand, these prerequisites have been met, an environment conducive to the assertive exercise of bargaining power exists.

Bargaining power, according to James Caporaso, is "the power to control the outcome of specific events."[12] Applied to the postdependency paradigm being developed here, it can be seen as an LDC's ability to negotiate the terms of its relationships with others, particularly the metropolitan centers to which it was traditionally subordinate. Indeed the capacity to do this is perhaps the most critical test of whether a Third World nation can legitimately be said to have acquired effective sovereignty. Yet even when the response is affirmative, this hardly means that the prerogatives involved are absolute; effective sovereignty is not synonymous with blanket autonomy. To the contrary, the developing country's foreign ties will in many respects continue to be asymmetrical, especially when operating on the North-South plane, where it will almost invariably be the weaker party and therefore will not enjoy the luxury of being able to bargain from a position of relative strength. Nevertheless, having reduced its vulnerabilities through diversification, an LDC should find the situation rather amenable to manipulating or renegotiating its external linkages in such a manner as to produce mutually beneficial rather than zero-sum configurations.

There are, of course, other factors that can contribute to a Third World government's bargaining power and thereby allow it to be a more proactive practitioner of postdependency politics. Among the internal traits influencing the capacity to execute counterdependency strategies successfully are, says John Ravenhill,

> the mobilizable economic resources of a country. . . . In addition, it is necessary to consider political and social variables such as the skills (and thus bargaining capability) of the domestic bureaucracy and the ability of the state to impose unpopular domestic policies on relevant domestic sectors who must bear the costs involved in capital accumulation (which would involve inter alia a consideration of the coercive capacity of the domestic government, its legitimacy, and its ability to mobilize the necessary constellation of class forces).[13]

Moving out into the international realm, a developing country may occasionally possess unusual bargaining power because the center is strategically dependent on it (e.g., industrialized nation A relies heavily on Third World country B to supply the wherewithal necessary for A's continued prosperity and future growth). In practice, however, it is extremely rare to find such fundamental weaknesses on which LDCs can capitalize. Consequently, a more realistic approach for them would be to try to strengthen their hands by negotiating collectively. Some forays in this direction have already been launched, the mechanisms employed ranging from regional vehicles (a good example in the Western Hemisphere being SELA—the Latin American Economic System) to commodity cartels (OPEC; the International Bauxite Association) to large, multiissue organizations with worldwide memberships (the Group of 77; the Movement of Nonaligned Nations). A common problem such multilateral initiatives have had to confront is the fact that the participants have not always been able to arrive at a consensus regarding their overall priorities, the result being serious susceptibility to retaliatory divide-and-conquer tactics as disgruntled members become increasingly prone to break ranks and make their separate peaces with the metropole. Conversely, the benefits that the CARICOM and other developing states have achieved within the Lomé framework (which is discussed further in the next chapter) suggests that, despite its faults, collective bargaining has immense potential as a means for LDCs to make major progress toward maximizing controlled dependence and thereby completing the first stage in the postdependency process.

Structural Power and Balanced Interdependence: The Ultimate Goals of Postdependency Politics

Making and especially consolidating the shift from dependency to controlled dependence obviously is a landmark accomplishment for any Third World nation that succeeds in doing so. The downside, of course, is the temptation to rest on one's laurels. Such a reaction would be quite understandable, since these system state transitions usually occur in a gradual, incremental fashion, which from a pragmatic economic or political perspective means that no similar triumphs could be anticipated in the near future and hence there would be little concrete motivation to plunge immediately back into the fray. However, switching from the behavioral to the theoretical plane, it must be understood that the assertive use of negotiating leverage is only one element, albeit a critical one, in a much larger universe wherein balanced interdependence represents the Holy Grail sought by all true pilgrims who embark on the long, arduous odyssey of postdependency politics. Accordingly, those developing countries that wish to carry the struggle for effective sovereignty to its limits cannot be satisfied with just maximizing their bargaining power within a context of controlled dependence, but rather must push on in a quest to obtain what Caporaso calls structural power, which is "the ability to manipulate the choices, capabilities, alliance opportunities, and payoffs that actors may utilize. Creating a producer cartel is structural power, for while that act itself is not a triumph over an opponent, it decreases the number of independent supply sources of consuming countries. . . . We say that this is a higher form of power because it is a power to *govern the rules* which shape bargaining power."[14] Stated a bit differently, structural power entails the capacity to redefine the fundamental dynamics of the interactions between two or more nations, thereby conferring on those who possess it the potential to wield a very high degree of control over their destinies. The implications involved with regard to Third World counterdependency aspirations are both obvious and enormous. With such clout the prospects would be favorable for instigating a process of drastic change in LDC relationships with the industrialized metropole, which could eventually produce a situation characterized by balanced interdependence. Without it the prospects for moving beyond controlled dependence are almost nonexistent.

The pursuit and acquisition of structural power constitutes the second main stage, henceforth referred to as protointerdependence, in the postdependency paradigm. Unfortunately, despite the fact that it is a distinct system state in the counterdependency scenario, protointerdependence is susceptible to being accorded minimal conceptual significance, since some might perceive it as little more than an inconsequential way station on the road to the promised land of balanced interdependence. While there is admittedly a kernel of practical truth to this viewpoint, it nevertheless is crucial to recognize that the specific impact on the evolving linkages between Third World nations and the larger global community that structural power can have is heavily dependent on whether one is at the point of simply getting it or actually using it. During the procurement (or protointerdependence) phase the prevailing pattern of foreign affairs will be maintained pretty much intact; no major changes in the overall configuration of the international order or in the relative placement of states within it can be expected. But it is quite a different story when those who have accumulated structural power begin to exploit it, for then one has moved beyond protointerdependence to the highest plateau of postdependency politics—balanced interdependence.

The effect that wielding structural power can have on the exact form that balanced interdependence assumes might be likened to the operation of a kaleidoscope. Applying a small amount of torque will produce some alterations in a few components. Increase that pressure, however, and a threshold is eventually reached where the modifications are so pervasive that an entirely new pattern emerges. The first of these two examples can be seen as being somewhat analogous to a single developing country using its newly acquired influence to improve and strengthen its station within the existing global arena. In other words, what occurs in this instance is status adjustment; structural power is employed to bring about changes that are limited to transforming the status or role of a particular nation in such a way as to assure that balanced interdependence is the norm in its relations with the outside world. The international system's essential nature thus has not been altered, but rather only the posture therein of certain states. On the other hand, when structural power is used by or in the interests of the periphery as a whole, the result may very well be a comprehensive systemic transformation comparable to the total reorganization that can be induced among the constituent parts of a kaleidoscope. When such a metamorphosis occurs what has transpired is not just another system state transition, but instead one of the rarest of all social phenomena—structural change resulting in a completely new system. The insistence on the need for an NIEO is perhaps the best contemporary manifestation of the Third World's desire for such a radical renovation of the global status quo.

The successful utilization of structural power stands as the final stage in this postdependency paradigm. Once such a shift was completed, developing countries would find themselves, either singularly or collectively, in the enviable position of being able to say that the serious vulnerabilities that once plagued their relationships with the industrialized countries have for the most part been eliminated and replaced by a network of positive sensitivities that should produce substantial mutual benefits for everyone involved.

The four-stage model utilized here to develop the concept of postdependency politics is schematically summarized in Figure 2.1. Note that the procedures illustrated in Figure 2.1 indicate that an ongoing process of status adjustment affecting a large number of LDCs could ultimately generate a systemic transformation. However, because most Third World leaders tend to be impatient when dealing with dependency-related matters (as illustrated by their demands for an NIEO in the very near future), the likelihood is that they would be more inclined to try to achieve quick fixes through multilateral initiatives rather than being content to wait for the phenomenon of cumulative status adjustment to run its protracted, circuitous course. In any case such considerations must (despite their intrinsic interest and importance) now be put aside in order to concentrate on the main topic at hand—exploring the South-South option's potential as a viable CARICOM strategy for pursuing controlled dependence.

Strategies of Postdependency Politics

While one could conceivably generate a wide range of postdependency strategies by focusing on the subtle individual nuances that characterize the policies and behavior of various Third World states, it can in a general sense be said that four main options exist with respect to making the transition from dependency to controlled dependence (and beyond): (1) supercliency; (2) the Singapore developmental model; (3) collective clientelism; and (4) the South-South approach. The scenario espoused by many radical dependentistas, which stresses comprehensive social revolutions in LDCs as the necessary and immediate precursors of structural changes at the international level, is not included on this list because, unlike the others, it does not conceptualize counterdependency dynamics in terms of movement through several system states, but rather looks on the process in terms of an almost cataclysmic shift from unmitigated dependency to systemic transformation. While such quantum leaps are, of course, conceivable theoretically, they rarely occur in practice and, in any case, stand outside the stage progression paradigm being used here. Consequently, the following

Figure 2.1 The Dependency-Postdependency Continuum

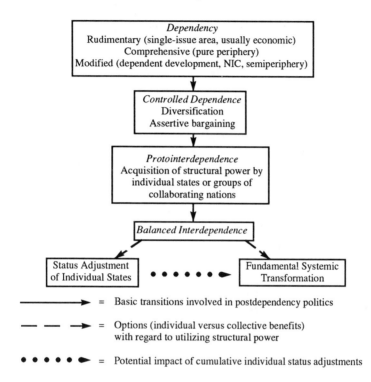

Dependency
Rudimentary (single-issue area, usually economic)
Comprehensive (pure periphery)
Modified (dependent development, NIC, semiperiphery)

Controlled Dependence
Diversification
Assertive bargaining

Protointerdependence
Acquisition of structural power by
individual states or groups of
collaborating nations

Balanced Interdependence

Status Adjustment
of Individual States

Fundamental Systemic
Transformation

———————▶ = Basic transitions involved in postdependency politics

— — —▶ = Options (individual versus collective benefits)
with regard to utilizing structural power

• • • • •▶ = Potential impact of cumulative individual status adjustments

material does not address the radical perspective, concentrating instead on briefly summarizing and evaluating the superclient, Singapore, and collective clientelism alternatives before turning to an in-depth examination of South-South relations as a postdependency vehicle for the CARICOM nations.

The Superclient Option

The superclient concept, which has been popularized by David Ronfeldt,[15] holds that occasionally a developing nation can, because of its strategic location or other factors, become such a valuable asset to a great power that it is able to extract significant concessions (including considerable decisionmaking flexibility in both the external and internal realms) from its patron, accomplishing all this despite the fact that it might appear to be locked into a dependency relationship. For example, during the Cold War some superclients tried to create political space for themselves not through the mechanisms of a nonaligned foreign policy and diversification, but rather by adopting a highly partisan posture on the global stage that allowed them to capitalize on and manipulate the competition between the United States and the Soviet Union. Thus what might have started as a classical core-periphery configuration became transformed, either by the evolutionary dynamics of the situation or the counterdependency initiatives of the LDC, into something more akin to a junior-senior partnership.

In certain respects, supercliency is similar to the idea of strategic dependency discussed in Chapter 1. However, whereas strategic dependency emphasizes the resource and related economic vulnerabilities of complex, highly developed industrial societies that can be exploited by Third World states, the superclient perspective stresses the military-political "services" a developing country can furnish, the most controversial being that of a surrogate in a particular region for the armed forces of a superpower. Cuba is the most frequently cited example of a Russian superclient, with Israel, and Iran under the shah, often being accorded similar status in the U.S. camp.[16]

The postdependency potential of the superclient option is in some respects rather impressive and in others quite constrained. Certainly its capacity to generate the bargaining power required by an LDC to make and consolidate the transition to controlled dependence without assuming the risks associated with the delinkage or diversification approach cannot be denied. Nor should the concrete material rewards involved be underestimated, for supercliency implies that, in addition to the gain of greater decisionmaking autonomy, extraordinary amounts of economic and military aid will be forthcoming from the metropole. On the downside, however, the prospects for acquiring structural power within a superclient framework are slim to nonexistent. Thus one cannot expect to proceed, using this strategy, very far across the total spectrum of postdependency politics. Moreover, the harsh reality is that there are few developing nations (and probably none in the English-speaking Caribbean) that possess the unique combination of strategic location and indigenous capabilities that, along with the totally fortuitous variable of facilitating circumstances, is necessary in order to be considered serious candidates for such a role. Thus, since the most that can be expected is some limited improvement within the existing system of global inequities for a very few countries, the superclient option does not appear to be a viable postdependency vehicle for the CARICOM states in particular, or for the Third World in general.

The Singapore Option

The *Singapore option* is a generic term applied to the success that several small Asian territories (Hong Kong and Taiwan as well as Singapore) have had in rapidly achieving rather high overall growth rates by adopting an export-oriented developmental model revolving around light consumer rather than heavy industrial enterprises. Viewed from a counterdependency perspective that assumes some opportunities for Third World nations to modernize within the context of existing core-periphery relationships, the most immediate goal is to acquire the economic capabilities necessary to implement selective delinkage and vertical diversification. In Singapore's case, its traditional British connection was the main focus of delinkage, while the United States was its primary vehicle for diversification. But whatever the specific dynamics involved may be, it is hoped that the economic and political space acquired through such a "break-out process" will, if properly exploited, translate into a fairly high degree of assertive bargaining power. In short, the Singapore option is a classic example of an incremental formula designed to allow its users to first modify their dependency status (i.e., become a part of the NIC contingent in the semiperiphery) and ultimately to make a system state transition to controlled dependence. Central to this scenario for those small Asian countries, which some have called "the little dragons,"[17] is the symbiotic interplay between the inherent competitive edge they enjoy as the result of their modest overhead costs and the substantial subsidies or services their governments have extended to the private sector. Basically, says Bernard Headley,

> low wages and a disciplined work force [have] allowed them to manufacture light goods more cheaply than could the industrialized West. As a means of spurring local companies to look to foreign markets, import barriers were lowered and liberal export incentives established. To obtain the capital needed for expansion, the governments of those countries lured foreign investment with generous tax holidays and the promise of cheap labor.[18]

In many instances this strategy has allowed its practitioners to gain a solid share in certain sectors of the metropolitan markets, with the United States naturally being the most lucrative target. In essence, then, the Singapore approach, rather than concerning itself with promoting basic changes in the prevailing global economic order (as advocated by NIEO enthusiasts), concentrates on manipulating the existing system effectively enough to insure one's acceptance, despite natural resource deficiencies and other obstacles, as a junior member of the international trading elite.

Although the Singapore phenomenon has attracted widespread interest and often intense admiration in the CARICOM area, it has yet to be fully transplanted there. The most ambitious attempt to do so was undertaken by Edward Seaga's government in Jamaica, with Ronald Reagan's administration providing strong support through its Caribbean Basin Initiative (CBI) program. Seeing the conservative Seaga's 1980 electoral landslide as a golden opportunity to discredit the leftist developmental scheme his predecessor, the democratic socialist Michael Manley, had tried unsuccessfully to implement, the White House enthusiastically embraced the new regime in Kingston. U.S. economic assistance flowed in on an unprecedented scale, escalating from $12.7 million to a peak of $136.9 million in 1982 (thereby making the island at that point second only to Israel in terms of per capita U.S. developmental aid). Subsequently these figures steadily declined, dropping to $93.9 million in 1988 and $72.6 million in 1989. Nevertheless, the overall total during the 1980s was an immense investment on Washington's part. Yet despite such generosity, Jamaica was not destined to become a Caribbean Singapore. Instead, having seen several promising spurts of progress run quickly out of steam, it found itself wallowing in the economic doldrums as Reagan left office in early 1989. Indeed there were even strong indications that the island had in some respects actually traveled in the wrong direction, the most dramatic being that it had by late 1988 achieved the dubious distinction of possessing one of the world's highest per capita foreign debts.[19]

Among the many obstacles confronting such efforts to replicate the East Asian experience, special concern has been voiced about infrastructural deficiencies, the basic contention being that most CARICOM countries (unlike their Oriental counterparts at a similar moment) do not have the transportation, communication, energy, and related capabilities that are prerequisites for achieving takeoff in the highly competitive world economy. Moreover, say these observers, there is little reason to believe that either the public or private sectors in the Caribbean will be able in the foreseeable future to raise the capital necessary to alleviate these problems. Even more important, however, are some fundamental differences in the sociopolitical cultures of the two regions. Historically, deference to centralized authority (both governmental and economic) has been the norm in the little dragons. Consequently labor unions have been weak. In the Anglophone Caribbean, on the other hand, the tradition of institutionalized opposition to existing power centers has remained strong; rival political parties flourish within the friendly confines of England's legacy of Westminster parliamentarianism, and militant labor movements are well entrenched, with many politicians combining the two threads by initially achieving prominence through their union connections and activities. In short, the dynamics of CARICOM societies have not been conducive to the emergence of the "disciplined" work forces so crucial to the success of the Asian model.[20]

Despite its questionable applicability in the English-speaking Caribbean, the Singapore scenario theoretically can serve as a vehicle for negotiating the various phases of the counterdependency process, the most likely outcome being status adjustment for those who utilize it effectively. The problem from a larger Third World standpoint is that such scenarios are not likely to be very numerous, since many countries do not possess the special sociocultural traits necessary to take advantage of whatever developmental prospects may be available, which in any case could prove to be somewhat fleeting because of fortuitous factors that can often produce relatively quick changes in global trade and other patterns. In short, the window of opportunity may be open for only a short time. Thus the odds seem to be rather slim that the Singapore approach could generate a fundamental systemic transformation (e.g., an NIEO) that would benefit the developing nations as a whole. It is this limited potential for broad-based structural change that renders the Singapore option dubious as macrostrategy for postdependency politics.

Collective Clientelism

Collective clientelism, according to John Ravenhill,

> refers to a relationship in which a group of weak states combine in an effort to exploit the special ties that link them to a more powerful state or group of states. Through this means they hope to construct an exclusive regime under which they exert a claim on the stronger party in order to preserve or gain particularistic advantages not available to nonassociated states. . . . For the weaker party, the intention . . . is to take advantage of a dialectic of dependency: to exploit their present dependence and special ties in order to gain resources that facilitate a future lessening of dependency.[21]

Basically, then, this concept entails a process of horizontal collaboration in order to acquire a degree of bargaining power sufficient to allow a collection of individually weak Third World countries to establish a relationship of controlled dependence on the North-South axis. Although these vertical linkages could theoretically be limited to a single industrialized nation, it is much more likely that a number of metropoles would become involved, especially if they are already members of an existing multilateral organization with which the developing states are attempting to establish a privileged connection. Probably the foremost example of such an arrangement is the Lomé Conventions, a series of agreements between the EC and a large number of ex-colonial African, Caribbean, and Pacific countries (i.e., the ACP Group) that give the Third World signatories preferred access to EC markets as well as guaranteeing them an unusual degree of price stability for the commodities they sell to Europeans. Economic aid provisions have also been incorporated into the packages. Protracted negotiations finally produced the first Lomé Convention in 1975, with revised versions being adopted in 1980, 1985, and 1990 following extensive (and sometimes rather heated) EC–ACP haggling.

Collective clientelism can to some degree be likened to a patron system wherein the junior partners not only profit from the material rewards flowing from the concessions they have been given, but are also afforded protection against fortuitous shifts in the international economic winds and irresponsible behavior by other major actors (including a benefactor who might otherwise pursue policies detrimental to their interests). The main difference, of course, is that rather than leaving the client solely dependent on someone else's goodwill, as is the case with a conventional godfather, collective clientelism provides an opportunity for the foot soldiers to play an active role in determining exactly what their benefits will be. Energizing this whole process is southern multilateralism, for through it a synergism is, it is hoped, created whereby individual LDCs that normally would not be deemed economically important by the industrialized countries can on the basis of their group identity assume the status of significant raw materials suppliers and perhaps even be seen as a component of a potentially lucrative mass market. While allowing the Third World to bargain from a position of increased strength, such a situation should also prove advantageous to industrialized nations by opening up a much broader and more stable range of trade and investment opportunities than would be available if they relied exclusively on a bilateral approach in their North-South relations.

The collective clientelism concept has been attacked, especially by radical dependentistas, as nothing more than a glorified version of modified dependency, the only novel aspect being that group rather than individual travel is presented as the best means for small states to make the move from the heart of the periphery to the promised land of dependent development. As such, collective clientelism is not seen as a viable counterdependency option, but rather as just a mechanism for trading one kind of subservience for another. Responding to such accusations, at least with regard to the Lomé Conventions, Ravenhill contends that collective clientelism

> is not synonymous with a strategy of "associated dependent development." The latter refers to a development policy based on encouraging investment by transnational corporations (TNCs) and exploiting the technological, financial, organizational, and market connections TNCs can provide to take advantage of changes in the international division of labor. While collective clientelism, as represented by the Lomé relationship, might have been expected to facilitate a strategy of this type, . . . this strategy was attractive to only a small minority of the more developed ACP states; . . . the majority were more interested in an insurance arrangement that would not *oblige* them to pursue any particular foreign economic policy.[22]

Admittedly, the distinctions involved are quite subtle, and a strong case can be made that collective clientelism does indeed equal modified dependency. Yet fairness and accuracy demand that the clientelist option be recognized as a legitimate counterdependency ploy because of its emphasis on horizontal collaboration as an effective way for LDCs to amass substantial negotiating leverage. But having made this concession, it likewise must be stressed that the utilization of such influence marks the outer boundaries of collective clientelism. In other words, its operative parameters are limited to the system state of controlled dependence; there is no serious interest in continuing onward to the structural power phase. In fact, the more successful its practitioners are in consolidating collective clientelism, the lower the probability that they will be inclined to explore other postdependency avenues. What is more likely to occur is a trade-off whereby the long-term goal of bringing about fundamental systemic change is jettisoned in favor of maximizing the immediate fruits of controlled dependence. Moreover, the lack of vertical diversification implied in this approach is potentially hazardous. Ideally, bargaining power should be employed in a manner that optimizes the range of North-South linkages available to Third World states and thereby assures the greatest possible flexibility in periodically reconfiguring these relationships. The clientelist tendency, however, is to put all your eggs in one basket by trying to arrange a comprehensive package deal with a single metropolitan center, which will persist (perhaps with some occasional modifications) over a long period of time. There are, to be sure, advantages to this strategy, the primary one being that it provides a sense of both psychological and material security by removing much of the uncertainty that developing nations often must face when sailing alone in the tumultuous seas of the international economy. The danger is that they may very well find themselves highly vulnerable, either singularly or as a group, to regressing back into dependency. These shortcomings lead inevitably to the conclusion that collective clientelism simply cannot address such larger and crucial issues as the Third World's deeply embedded aspirations for an NIEO and therefore does not in the final analysis have much to offer those seeking a blueprint for running the entire gauntlet of postdependency politics.

The South-South Scenario

The South-South option shares certain characteristics with the collective self-reliance concept discussed in Chapter 1. In both cases, there is at the tactical level a heavy emphasis on markedly increasing the flow of investment capital, technology, trade, and even aid between LDCs, thereby, it is hoped, strengthening their joint capability to achieve significant socioeconomic progress. In particular, a major concern is to determine the best fit among nations with regard to their human and natural resources in order to create the economies of scale (both in terms of productive facilities and markets) normally associated with high rates of growth. It is, however, recognized that such exercises, no matter how far removed from the political arena in a purely technocratic sense, do not and cannot occur in a power vacuum. Thus attention is also devoted within each perspective to the question of Third World vulnerability to external penetration and domination. Both see horizontal collaboration as an essential first step for delinking developing countries from existing patterns of dependency, and both likewise realize that once this has been accomplished new patterns of North-South ties will have to be established, with the most likely profile entailing negotiations by groups of LDCs in an effort to create a diversified network of developmental relationships with multiple centers of metropolitan power. In essence, then, the immediate goal of both the South-South and collective self-reliance approaches to postdependency politics is to acquire the political and economic space, and the bargaining power, necessary for the LDCs to be able to exert some coordinated command over their dealings with the already highly modernized nations within an ongoing context of North-South interdependence and Third World sensitivities. In other words, the short-term target of each approach is controlled dependence.

At this point, however, some very important theoretical and conceptual differences emerge. Specifically, collective self-reliance is geared toward autarky; its best-case projections foresee LDCs exploiting their resource interface so effectively that they will be able to reach the takeoff point for self-sustained development. They will, in short, have gained the maximum effective sovereignty possible, at least with respect to the North-South axis, on which interdependence would no longer be seen as a major consideration. Within this framework, bargaining power clearly is devalued and may even be viewed as almost useless, since its key function—to facilitate vertical diversification of the South's relations with the North—is not relevant to the priority items on the collective self-reliance agenda. Such ideas do not, to say the least, make much sense to South-South devotees. They reject as hopelessly naive the contention that any significant degree of southern autonomy can be achieved on either an individual or multilateral basis. Such aspirations, while admittedly desirable in the abstract, are dismissed as being incompatible with the harsh realities (which cannot be expected to change any time soon) of the international environment. Consequently, heavy stress is placed on the notion that North-South interdependence is inevitable, which in turn implies concentrating on trying to arrange it in a manner optimally beneficial to the Third World.

Basically, and as opposed to the collective self-reliance approach where delinkage tends to be viewed as the ultimate goal because it translates into self-reliance, the South-South paradigm advocates relinkage within a more favorable context. The driving force behind this dialectic is power, with the exact configuration of relinkage being dependent on the kind of clout that horizontal collaboration has generated; the bargaining variety leads to controlled dependence, while its structural counterpart can produce balanced interdependence. Horizontal collaboration is therefore not perceived as a passport to some brave new self-reliant world, but rather as a means to procure the leverage required to alter the global political-economic environment within which the developing countries will pursue their quest for modernization, the process being recognized as a sequential one wherein a series of specific system state changes (involving increased levels of effective sovereignty at each stage) need to be made.

Flowing from these theoretical and conceptual distinctions are certain policy implications, the most important being that the South-South perspective tends to produce a much more coherent macrostrategy for launching postdependency initiatives than does the collective self-reliance model. The South-South option clearly pinpoints the various phases of the postdependency continuum and provides rather definitive guidelines regarding what kinds of action must be taken to acquire the specific capabilities (e.g., bargaining or structural power) required to make the transitions. The collective self-reliance school, on the other hand, tends to project a quantum leap from dependency to (utopian?) self-reliance without providing a detailed road map. Hence there will probably be an inclination to try to operationalize collective self-reliance by simply seizing on any opportunity for Third World cooperation that becomes available. The danger, of course, is that such an approach may degenerate into a haphazard, disjointed patchwork of ties that produce little in the way of broad-based, coordinated counterdependency offensives and that may even function at cross-purposes, thereby creating an ironic and perhaps even tragic situation where, like the character in Walt Kelly's "Pogo," the developing nations discover that "we have met the enemy and he is us."

The horizontal diversification and cooperation called for in South-South politics can operate at three basic levels—or maybe the analogy of three concentric circles would be more appropriate.

1. Working outward from the innermost ring, we start with basic regional, the most common manifestation of which is an economic integration movement that usually encompasses a fairly limited number of participants who share a particular regional identity. The best examples in the English-speaking Caribbean are CARICOM and the Organization of Eastern Caribbean States (OECS). Theoretically, a bilateral LDC link could also be included in this category, but such partnerships generally do not receive much attention or encouragement because the essential thrust of the South-South approach is toward multilateralism.

2. The interregional circle might in some instances also be termed *macroregional*. "Macroregional" refers to those experiments in integration or cooperation that cast their net broadly and, perhaps more salient, often incorporate existing institutions that are more narrowly based. SELA, which in a certain sense seeks to consolidate and build on the efforts of such predecessors as the Central American Common Market, the Andean Group, and even CARICOM, epitomizes this genre in the Western Hemisphere. "Interregional," of course, should be self-explanatory, a classical group here

being OPEC, since it draws its membership from the Middle East, sub-Saharan Africa, Latin America, and Southeast Asia.[23]

3. The global ring involves efforts to develop large-scale associations wherein practically all developing nations are represented. The two most widely known and successful forays into this territory are the Group of 77 (G-77, which, despite its name, actually has approximately 125 LDCs participating) and the Movement of Nonaligned Nations (NAM). G-77 devotes practically all its energy to developmental issues, while the NAM tends to be somewhat more oriented toward achieving foreign policy coordination on political and security matters such as the Palestinian question, apartheid in South Africa, and the crisis that destabilized Central America throughout the 1980s. There is, however, also an economic component in the NAM's agenda, as reflected in its desire to promote the NIEO idea and its efforts to develop a consensus regarding the best way to resolve the Third World debt problem.

In each of these theaters of operation, just as is the case with the other three counterdependency options discussed here, the most immediate concern is to make and consolidate the initial system state transition to controlled dependence. But beyond this particular shared characteristic, the South-South approach takes on dimensions much broader and more ambitious than any of its counterparts. For instance, in contrast to the superclient and collective clientelism concepts, which tend to define postdependency politics primarily in terms of the transformation to controlled dependence, the South-South model sees this phenomenon as merely the first step that needs to be taken in altering the LDCs' station in the international community. Once this has been achieved, attention shifts almost immediately to proceeding to the next stage, protointerdependence. Admittedly, the Singapore paradigm operates on the same agenda to this point. But then it too assumes a distinctive personality based on its propensity to accord to status adjustment a higher priority than to structural change. In other words, the question of systemic transformation is finessed by focusing instead on the graduation of individual developing nations to NIC or some other similar position within the existing international political-economic framework. The South-South approach, on the other hand, comes directly to grips with the structural macrochallenge, seeking to serve as the catalyst for a process whereby the North-South relations of the Third World as a whole will be so radically (and beneficially) altered that an entirely new global order will emerge. Epitomizing this audacity is the heavy premium that South-South devotees place on the need for an NIEO; none of the other viewpoints analyzed here exhibits a comparable commitment.

Thus, when all the variables and dimensions involved are considered the South-South option stands alone as the only truly comprehensive approach to postdependency politics. Indeed even the Cubans, traditionally the most fervent advocates in the Caribbean Basin of revolutionary rather than evolutionary change, have incorporated some aspects of its incremental multilateralism into their foreign policies. If such allegedly inflexible radicals as the Fidelistas can succumb to the lure of what is clearly a moderate, gradualistic counterdependency strategy that places much greater stress on maximizing flexibility than on maintaining ideological purity, one should hardly be surprised to find similar proclivities among the pragmatists who tend to dominate the political arena in the CARICOM countries.

Notes

1. See Morton Kaplan, *System and Process in International Politics* (New York: John Wiley and Sons, 1957), ch. 2.
2. Some examples of this line of analysis are in Keith Orton and George Modelski, "Dependency Reversal: National Attributes and Systemic Processes"; and Cal Clark and Donna Barry, "Dependency in the Soviet Bloc: A Reversal of the Economic-Political Nexus." (Both papers were presented at the 1979 annual conference of the International Studies Association, Toronto, Ontario).
3. Robert Keohane and Joseph Nye, "International Interdependence and Integration," in Paul Viotti and Mark Kauppi, eds., *International Relations Theory: Realism, Pluralism, Globalism* (New York: Macmillan, 1987), p. 366.
4. Alberto van Klaveren, "The Analysis of Latin American Foreign Policies: Theoretical Perspectives," in Heraldo Muñoz and Joseph S. Tulchin, eds., *Latin American Nations in World Politics* (Boulder, CO: Westview Press, 1984), p. 9.
5. James A. Caporaso, "Dependence, Dependency, and Power in the Global System: A Structural and Behavioral Analysis," *International Organization* 32, no. 1 (Winter 1978):18.
6. James N. Rosenau, "Pre-Theories and Theories of Foreign Policy," in R. Barry Farrell, ed., *Approaches to Comparative and International Politics* (Evanston, IL: Northwestern University Press, 1966), p. 65 (emphasis in original). For more details regarding the concept and the dynamics of penetrated systems, see ibid., pp. 60–71.
7. Hans A. Mouritzen, "Defensive Acquiescence: Making the Best Out of Dependence," in Otmar Höll, ed., *Small States in Europe and Dependence* (Boulder, CO: Westview Press, 1983), pp. 239–261.
8. Ole Elgström, "Active Foreign Policy as a Preventive Strategy Against Dependence," in Höll, *Small States*, pp. 262–280.
9. William Demas, *Consolidating Our Independence: The Major Challenge for the West Indies* (Distinguished Lecture Series, Institute of International Relations, University of the West Indies, Republic of Trinidad and Tobago, 1986), p. 23.
10. Bengt Sundelius, "Coping with Structural Security Threats," in Höll, *Small States*, p. 295.
11. For more information regarding the extremely varied field of game theory, see such representative contributions as Thomas Schelling, *The Strategy of Conflict* (New York: Oxford University Press, 1960); Martin Shubik, *Games for Society, Business, and War: Towards a Theory of Gaming* (New York: Elsevier Press, 1975); Steven H. Brams, *Game Theory and Politics* (New York: Free Press, 1975); and

Glenn H. Snyder and Paul Diesing, *Conflict Among Nations: Bargaining, Decision-Making, and System Structure in International Crises* (Princeton, NJ: Princeton University Press, 1977).

12. James A. Caporaso, "Introduction to the Special Issue of *International Organization* on Dependence and Dependency in the Global System," *International Organization* 32, no. 1 (Winter 1978): 4.

13. John Ravenhill, *Collective Clientelism: The Lomé Conventions and North-South Relations* (New York: Columbia University Press, 1985), p. 8.

14. Caporaso, "Introduction," p. 4 (emphasis added).

15. See David Ronfeldt, *Superclients and Superpowers: Cuba/Soviet Union and Iran/United States* (Santa Monica, CA: Rand Corporation, 1978).

16. As one might expect, controversy and acrimony have swirled around the superclient concept. Countries that have been so labeled have vehemently denied playing any such role, looking on the whole exercise as nothing more than an insulting and transparent attempt to smear them as puppets. Similarly, serious disagreements have often erupted among both academics and policymakers regarding the model's usefulness in describing the nature and dynamics of particular relationships, with perhaps the best example in the United States being the debate that has raged over the extent to which Cuba can be accurately perceived as a Soviet military surrogate in Africa and the Caribbean Basin.

17. This term is used by James Lee Ray (*Global Politics,* 3d ed. [Boston: Houghton Mifflin, 1987], p. 261) within the context of an excellent short summary of dependency theory and national developmental strategies. Ray discusses the extent to which the Singapore experience challenges and even in some instances supports various aspects of conventional *dependencia* wisdom.

18. Bernard D. Headley, "Beyond a Manley Victory in Jamaica," *Monthly Review* 38, no. 9 (February 1987): 24.

19. For information and analysis regarding these economic developments in Jamaica, see John Hickey, "The Stabilization Program of the United States in Jamaica," *Inter-American Economic Affairs* 37 (Autumn 1983): 63–72; Richard L. Bernal, "Foreign Investment and Development in Jamaica," *Inter-American Economic Affairs* 38 (Autumn 1984): 2–21; Anthony Thorndike, "Trade, Finance, and Politics: The Political Economy of Jamaica" (paper presented at the May 1987 conference of the Caribbean Studies Association, Belize City, Belize); and Evelyne Huber Stevens and John D. Stevens, "Manley Prepares to Return," *Caribbean Review* 16, no. 2 (Winter 1988): 16–19ff.

20. Two excellent analyses of the Singapore model's transferability to the English-speaking Caribbean are in Peter L. Berger, "Can the Caribbean Learn from East Asia? The Case of Jamaica," *Caribbean Review* 13, no. 2 (Spring 1984): 7–9ff.; and Bernardo Vega, "The CBI Faces Adversity: Lessons from the Asian Export Strategy," *Caribbean Review* 14, no. 2 (Spring 1985): 18–19ff.

21. Ravenhill, *Collective Clientelism,* pp. 22–23.

22. Ibid., p. 29 (emphasis in original).

23. The members of OPEC are Algeria, Iran, Iraq, Kuwait, Libya, Qatar, Saudi Arabia, the United Arab Emirates, Gabon, Nigeria, Ecuador, Venezuela, and Indonesia.

3

The Evolution of CARICOM
Postdependency Politics:
Exercising the South-South Option

The Caribbean Community displays all the characteristics normally associated with an organization operating at the first level of South-South politics: its membership is limited to those English-speaking nations that share a tradition of colonial ties to Great Britain; and it was conceived primarily as an instrument for regional integration, with heavy emphasis on promoting economic cooperation in order to stimulate and maintain developmental momentum within the group's individual countries. However, since an integral component of the CARICOM experiment involves attempting to coordinate its participants' foreign policies, it often serves as the mechanism West Indian states use to move collectively into the broader interregional and global realms of Third World affairs.

Individual Anglophone countries have, of course, sometimes pursued a unilateral South-South agenda, the two most prominent examples being Guyana under Forbes Burnham and Jamaica during Michael Manley's first administration (1972–1980). In general, however, the prevailing trend for the CARICOM states has been to try to present a united front when venturing out onto the world stage. Hence the main focus here will be on such multilateral initiatives.

CARICOM's Precursors:
The West Indies Federation and CARIFTA[1]

On August 2, 1956, after years of discussion in both the West Indies and London, the British Parliament endorsed the establishment of a federal union among its Caribbean colonies wherein power would be divided among a governor-general (representing the Crown), a council of state, and a bicameral legislature composed of a Senate and a House of Representatives. The House was the only component whose seats were to be filled through popular election; all other positions were appointive, with the governor-general playing a central role in the process. Indeed, ultimate executive authority rested to a great extent with the governor-general, who was given primary jurisdiction over defense, external relations, and matters concerning financial stability, as well as being empowered to disallow legislation dealing with other issues. The Federation of the West Indies formally came into existence on January 3, 1958, its ten members being Antigua, Barbados, Dominica, Grenada, Jamaica, Montserrat, St. Kitts–Nevis-Anguilla, St. Lucia, St. Vincent, and Trinidad and Tobago.

The Federation was plagued with difficulties and deficiencies from the very beginning. There was, for example, no provision or plans for a customs union, the result of Jamaica's opposition to lowering its extremely high tariffs and thereby opening its markets to various Caribbean competitors (particularly Trinidad and Tobago, which already had the lowest import duties in the group and therefore would not have to make concessions commensurate to Jamaica's). Such sensitivity over relative status was symptomatic of larger concerns generated by the wide disparity in economic and especially human resources among the participants. A certain imbalance is, of course, inevitable in any integration scheme. In the West Indian case, however, the configuration was unusually disequilibrated because Jamaica (population 1,609,800) and Trinidad and Tobago (population a little over 800,000) accounted for seven-eighths of the area's total citizenry and three-fourths of its aggregate wealth. These problems could perhaps have been ameliorated with strong leadership, but generally it was not forthcoming because individuals were prohibited from holding high political office at the national and regional levels simultaneously. Forced to make a choice, the Caribbean's most prominent and capable figures almost invariably opted to concentrate on consolidating their positions within their countries. Initially, however, such complications were not sufficient to derail the Federation's momentum. To the contrary, its proponents remained firmly convinced that integration was the only viable mechanism for the Caribbean countries to use in pursuing independence and attempting to create opportunities for their inhabitants to achieve a decent standard of living.

Unfortunately, the optimism of the early, halcyon days faded rather quickly. The lack of widespread commitment to leadership among the region's notables was driven home with depressing finality when it became time to choose the Federation's prime minister. The best-qualified candidates in practically everyone's eyes were Norman Manley of Jamaica, Dr. Eric Williams of Trinidad and Tobago, and Sir Grantley Adams of Barbados. But neither Manley nor Williams was inclined to forsake his established national power base to assume an office of uncertain authority in the regional government, thereby setting a precedent that prompted many of their colleagues to be leery of a career in federal politics. Grantley Adams was, however, willing to shoulder the responsibility and hence was appointed the first prime minister of the West Indies in early 1958.

The situation began to unravel seriously in 1960 as Jamaica became increasingly disgruntled with the Federation and began to consider withdrawing. Kingston's main concern, especially as its prospects for independence brightened, focused on its contention that the island's development could be hindered by its membership in the union, since actions affecting its economic future might very well be taken or inordinately influenced by nonnationals. This sentiment was a crucial element in Jamaica's decision to hold a referendum in 1961 to determine whether it would remain in the Federation. Despite the fact that the federal Constitution contained no provision or authorization for a member to secede, Kingston proceeded with the balloting. With only 60.8 percent of the registered voters actually participating, the rejectionist forces triumphed by a margin of 8.2 percent (54.1 supporting nonassociation and 45.9 opposing). Thus the death knell for the Federation of the West Indies was sounded, with Trinidad's Eric Williams delivering its epitaph in his famous comment that "ten minus one equals nothing." The official demise occurred on April 2, 1962, when a bill to dissolve was approved by the British House of Commons.

Despite the demise of the West Indies Federation, the snowballing momentum of decolonization,[2] in conjunction with increased awareness of the problems attendant on independence, functioned to maintain interest in the idea of Caribbean integration. In particular, as had occurred earlier in Latin America, there was growing sentiment that some form of collaboration had to be explored as a means to stimulate significant economic development and to minimize the prospects of serious external dependency (which was conceptualized in more radical circles as artificial sovereignty). Among the obstacles to modernization confronting the West Indian territories on which various observers focused heavily were the relatively sparse volume of interisland trade caused by tariff barriers, inadequate intraregional transportation and communication systems, and the lack of diversity in export products; the perpetuation of traditional trade patterns, with the Caribbean nations locked into the unenviable position of exchanging low-cost commodities such as sugar for expensive finished products produced by the more industrialized countries; and the divisive impact on the area associated with the operation of center-based multinational corporations.[3]

As informal discussions regarding the exact form a new integration scheme might take proceeded, two basic schools of thought emerged. The more ambitious, which tended to reflect the thinking of academics associated with the UWI, stressed the need to develop mechanisms for coordinating production activities within the region to assure that they would be complementary rather than duplicative. Such a strategy, it was felt, would not only generate the conditions and incentives for greater interisland commerce, but would also enhance the status of Caribbean nations as trading partners in the broader international economic system. The second perspective, which enjoyed solid support from many business elements (particularly in the larger nations), set its sights somewhat lower by focusing on the more conventional strategy of incremental tariff reductions in order to achieve over the long run a free trade area. This approach would, its advocates hoped, create markets of scale that would serve as incentives for major developmental commitments by both local and foreign investors.[4] But regardless of which proposal was on the table, the LDCs were very much worried that they might find themselves in the disadvantageous position of being forced to compete (both at home and regionally) with such powerful entities as Jamaica and Trinidad and Tobago. In theory, at least, an integrated production scenario has the capacity to address these concerns by establishing from the very beginning a clear-cut division of labor among its members that should serve to offset their resource disparities. Achieving such safeguards is, however, a much trickier proposition when operating within a free trade framework; while the assurances LDCs demand are conceptually inconsistent with the goal of an unrestricted flow of goods and services, pragmatism requires that some accommodations be made. Consequently, what usually emerges in such situations is a modified arrangement entailing a delicate counterbalance of political and economic considerations. This was, in essence, exactly what happened in the West Indies.

The December 1965 agreement among Antigua, Barbados, and Guyana to form a free trade area, which was to some extent stimulated by the possibility that Caribbean exports to Great Britain might lose their privileged status if London decided to join the European Economic Community (EEC),[5] was the first formal attempt to resuscitate the integration movement. Subsequently, working through the West Indies Associated States (WISA) Council of Ministers, which had been set up in 1966, seven of the miniislands (Antigua, Dominica, Grenada, Montserrat, St. Ketts–Nevis, St. Lucia, and St. Vincent) concluded a pact in April 1968 creating the Eastern Caribbean Common Market (ECCM). These initiatives in effect laid the foundation upon which the Caribbean Free Trade Association (CARIFTA) was built.

The overall outline for CARIFTA was drawn up at an August 1967 meeting in Georgetown, Guyana, attended by governmental officials, academics, and leading figures from the West Indian business community. Using the existing Antigua-Barbados-Guyana convention as their working model, the delegates concluded that the integration process should be expanded in accordance with the following general principles:

1. *Elimination of import duties and quotas in intraregional commerce.* Provisions were, however, included for the formulation of reserve lists that

would allow certain items to be exempted from such provisions for at least five or, in the case of some LDCs, seven years.

2. *Establishment of a Caribbean bank to help provide developmental capital, with particular attention being devoted to satisfying infrastructural requirements in the agricultural and tourism sectors*

3. *Organization of the institutional mechanisms (e.g., a regional secretariat) necessary to assure that the programs involved proceeded smoothly and efficiently*

These broad proposals, along with more specific supplementary suggestions, were accepted as the basis for CARIFTA at a Commonwealth Caribbean Heads of Government Conference in October 1967. CARIFTA became fully functional on August 1, 1968, its charter having been negotiated and ratified by all the WISA participants, Barbados, Guyana, Jamaica, and Trinidad and Tobago. Belize became its twelfth and last member in May 1971.[6]

CARIFTA was really a rather modest foray into the realm of multilateral cooperation; it did not, in the final analysis, seek to achieve a high level of integration among its members, preferring instead to concentrate almost exclusively on the more limited goal of removing constraints on intraregional commerce. Commenting on its fundamental nature and limitations, Andrew Axline notes that

> CARIFTA involved the elimination of barriers on products traded within the region. It did not free the movement of other factors of production (labor and capital) and thus was not a common market. It did not have a common external tariff and thus was not even a customs union. Although [CARIFTA's organizers] had recognized the problem of inequitable distribution of benefits, . . . there were no major distributive measures included. There were a number of provisions affecting the LDCs in such a way as to alter favorably the relationship between the costs and benefits of their participation, but most of them were "opting out" or escape-clause mechanisms which aimed to reduce costs rather than provide benefits.[7]

There was, of course, some interest in addressing larger developmental issues. For instance, the Caribbean Development Bank, while not a formal CARIFTA institution, was established to support the association's activities and to help provide investment capital (especially to the small islands that, given their minuscule size and narrow resource base, were expected to have trouble attracting outside money). Overall, then, what CARIFTA represented was a modified free trade arrangement rather than an ambitious blueprint for regional integration.

The major problem that CARIFTA faced was the LDCs' ongoing skepticism about the cost-benefit ratio of membership. In essence, they feared that the free trade regime would increase rather than lessen their vulnerability to being economically overwhelmed by their larger neighbors, these sentiments being a crucial factor behind their decision to establish the ECCM prior to joining CARIFTA. On the other hand, the almost inevitable loss of their privileged entry to the English market that would occur once the United Kingdom joined the EEC led them to conclude that they had no choice but to test the integration alternative. Unfortunately, the results were not satisfactory. Such cost-minimization safeguards as the reserve lists proved to be ineffective, and the situation was aggravated by the lack of any systematic mechanism to assure a rough parity in rewards. The balance sheets graphically illustrate these shortcomings and inequities: the share of regional commerce controlled by the larger countries (i.e., Barbados, Guyana, Jamaica, and Trinidad and Tobago) rose from 60 percent in 1967 to 69 percent in 1971 while during this same period trade among the LDCs themselves declined from 1.9 percent to 1.4 percent of the total activity within the CARIFTA area.[8] This track record, combined with growing sentiment among practically all the participants for a common external tariff, triggered an ongoing debate (which would eventually produce CARICOM) about the need to "deepen" the integration process.

Despite an awareness of the need to come to grips with the specter of dependency, neither the West Indies Federation nor CARIFTA exhibited any significant capacity to transform this perception into policy and practice. Realistically, one could not expect much postdependency progress from the Federation, since none of its members were independent states during its lifetime. Thus, in terms of dealing with the problem of external control, the issue at this time was defined mainly in terms of attaining formal sovereignty. In other words, their decolonization had to be completed before the Caribbean nations were in a position to elevate the struggle against neocolonialism to a prominent niche on their international agenda.

Even had the participants wanted to do so, the power structure of the West Indies Federation militated against counterdependency initiatives because the governor-general, who was appointed by and represented the British metropole, had primary jurisdiction over its members' foreign relations as well as the authority to block legislation in practically any issue-area. Given this heavy quotient of built-in exogenous authority, the Federation could hardly serve as a launching platform for vigorous antidependency offensives (especially any that might primarily target British interests or those of British allies). Admittedly, had the Caribbean nations actually become independent within the context of a strong regional union, the size-versus-viability dilemma would have been less severe and hence their degree of vulnerability to postcolonial dependency may have been reduced. However, since the Federation self-destructed prior to independence, the question is moot.

In CARIFTA's case the parameters of action that were established in conceptualizing the organization tended to exclude provisions conducive to the pursuit of postdependency politics. For example, the decision to forgo any serious efforts at integrating regional production removed the collective self-reliance strategy as an option in the CARIFTA repertoire. This approach to combatting dependency demands, as noted previously, utilization of the human and natural resources of certain countries to overcome the deficiencies of others, the ultimate goal being to generate a developmental synergism of significant proportions. Implicit in this paradigm is a high degree of economic planning, which was not a feature incorporated into CARIFTA. In a similar vein, CARIFTA's failure to confront the issue of establishing a common external tariff was an indication that it was not particularly concerned with developing or enhancing its bargaining power vis-à-vis the industrialized centers. Indeed, it devoted very little attention to the question of renegotiating its relations, economic or otherwise, with nations or areas outside the Caribbean. Instead, CARIFTA's main thrust was intraregional, revolving around the attempt to promote more commerce among the West Indian states through the mechanism of a free trade regime. Such factors and considerations combined to preclude any serious postdependency dimension to CARIFTA's organizational and operative personality.

CARICOM:
The Metamorphosis to a South-South Dimension

There was, of course, a wide range of factors that converged to produce a much more ambitious Caribbean integration agenda. Initially the most visible and influential catalyst for change was the technocratic lobby, which insisted that CARIFTA's modest free trade regime had essentially served its purpose as an incubator for regional cooperation and therefore it was now incumbent to move on to the next plateau—the creation of a common market revolving around a comprehensive system of uniform external tariffs and mechanisms to promote distributive justice for the LDCs. Such sentiments, which were to a great extent rooted in disillusionment with CARIFTA's track record, were undoubtedly the primary driving force behind the movement to explore new frontiers of collaboration; the effort would, in other words, almost certainly have been made even if other variables had not come into play, the two most important being the expanding EEC and the growing concern about postcolonial dependency.

The West Indies as well as practically all members of the British Commonwealth had always looked with considerable trepidation on the idea of London's entry into the European Common Market, for such a move would inevitably disrupt the existing economic arrangements that provided privileged access to the English market for many former British colonies. Indeed those special ties had been, by virtue of complicating the negotiations between London and the EEC over the terms of the United Kingdom's admission, one of the major obstacles to British participation. By the early 1970s, however, it had become clear that the marriage was a foregone conclusion and that the only substantive matter that had to be settled was the exact timing of the nuptials. The Caribbean countries were thus confronted with a situation that made it inevitable that their relations not only with England, but also Western Europe as a whole, would have to be redefined. The question therefore naturally arose regarding the best bargaining mode for pursuing such a reconfiguration. Clearly the bilateral option was very risky; the individual West Indian nations would, given their small size and limited economic influence, be operating from a position of considerable weakness and would be highly susceptible to divide-and-conquer tactics. A multilateral approach, while obviously preferable, was hindered by the fact that there was no existing organizational mechanism that could easily be activated once the time came to enter into negotiations. CARIFTA, of course, was not suited to such tasks; it was authorized to establish and administer a regional free trade regime, not to function as an agent for collective bargaining with the outside world. Thus the problem confronting Caribbean governments was whether to create an ad hoc negotiating body when it became necessary to confront the implications of London's association with the EEC or to establish a new vehicle that would be ready to assume such responsibilities as required. Increasingly the consensus tilted toward the latter alternative, which meant that CARIFTA would either have to be retooled or superseded by a body (such as CARICOM) with a much broader mandate.

Within this larger context of essentially technocratic and bureaucratic issues the more abstract dependency debate began to have a significant impact on political dialog in the West Indies. Concerns about structural vulnerability and sophisticated mechanisms of external control, which had previously been aired mainly within the academic community (where the work of Latin American *dependencia* theorists exerted considerable influence), now surfaced more regularly in the political arena as Caribbean nations either achieved or faced the imminent prospect of independence. As the postcolonial process evolved, says Anthony Bryan, "the dichotomy between political independence and the reality of economic dependence emerged. As had been happening almost a decade earlier in Latin America, concern was now directed toward external dependency and the need for regional economic integration as a means of accelerating economic development and minimizing this dependency."[9] Recognizing CARIFTA's meager ability to address the threat, some of its officials as well as representatives of West Indian governments organized a group in 1970 to explore what concrete steps might be taken in this direction. Their response, after two years of study and consultations, was a detailed elaboration of the area's need to adopt a unified approach with regard to controlling foreign investment and an outline of the specific provisions that should be incorporated into such a plan.[10] Such initiatives were symptomatic of the growing inclination to include the question of developing a collective counterdependency capability in any discussions about the future course of regional integration.

The uncertainty about CARIFTA's viability produced by the cumulative impact of criticisms or problems raised by the technocrats, EC–watchers, and dependency theorists, combined with dissatisfaction (especially among the smaller islands) over its economic performance, triggered a flurry of study groups, reports, and meetings geared to producing a blueprint for Caribbean integration that would push the movement to new levels of multidimensionality and sophistication. The crucial governmental negotiations in this process occurred at three Council of Ministers assemblies (in Dominica in July 1972, in Trinidad and Tobago in October 1972, and in Guyana in April 1973) and two Heads of Government conferences (in Trinidad and Tobago in October 1972 and in Guyana in April 1973).

The frustration that had been building in the LDC ranks over the lack of any effective means to assure a reasonably equitable distribution of cooperation's benefits quickly became apparent at the July 1972 Council of Ministers sessions in Dominica. Basically, what the LDCs demanded as the price for their participation in any future integration experiments was the acceptance of a quota system whereby they would be allocated 95 percent of all new industries established for serving the regional market and protected by uniform external tariffs. Needless to say, such a proposal was not enthusiastically embraced by the larger countries, whose primary interest was to create a strong West Indian common market by supplementing CARIFTA's free trade arrangements with a system of standardized customs duties. As it became obvious that these different priorities were not going to be resolved quickly given the conceptual chasms separating the various parties, the delegates decided to concentrate on sketching the broad outlines of a package deal by drawing up a list of core issues to be placed on the agendas of upcoming meetings. The main bargaining topics to emerge were common external tariffs (CETs); harmonization of fiscal investment incentives, especially those applying to outsiders; regional allocation of new industries; and a unified Caribbean approach to negotiations with the EC.

The ensuing diplomatic dance was intricate, encompassing a shifting cast of organizations and individuals seeking the right formula to dissolve the fault line separating the LDCs from the more developed countries. Ignoring the details of the two parties' evolving positions as the drama unfolded, the basic psychology and passions that came into play are illustrated by the following statements: "We of the less developed territories share the desire of other CARIFTA members for meaningful economic integration. But, our people want to see factories—they want to see visible benefits of CARIFTA" (James Mitchell, premier of St. Vincent and chairman of the LDC Caucus); "We cannot give blood as some representatives of the LDCs want. But it is in our interest and theirs to find a reasonable compromise" (Kamaluddin Mohammed, minister of West Indian Affairs, Trinidad and Tobago).[11] Slowly, however, a web of conciliation and cooperation was spun, the key advances emerging from the two October 1972 Trinidad meetings and the April 1973 Council conclave in Guyana.

The final chapter in the transition from CARIFTA to CARICOM was played out at the April 1973 Heads of Government Conference, where deals that had already been struck in previous discussions were ratified in a document that became known as the Georgetown Accord. Essentially an agreement to agree, the Accord provided that the four largest countries— Barbados, Guyana, Jamaica, and Trinidad and Tobago—would sign a pact creating the Caribbean Community in July 1973, which would then become operative on August 1, 1973. The remaining participants (i.e., the LDCs) would join no later than May 1, 1974. It was also stipulated that various treaties, of special interest to the smaller nations, dealing with harmonization of fiscal incentives to industry, avoidance of double taxation, and the establishment of a Caribbean Investment Corporation would be inaugurated on June 1, 1973. Pursuant to this two-stage timetable, the official birth of CARICOM occurred on July 4, 1973, when the Big Four gathered in Trinidad to sign the Treaty of Chaguaramas. Subsequently the eight LDCs would also become members, thereby completing the process of transforming CARIFTA into the Caribbean Common Market and Community.[12]

The mission CARICOM set for itself was basically threefold: to facilitate economic integration in the area; to promote functional collaboration in as many fields as possible; and to provide a mechanism for coordinating the foreign policies of its members. In postdependency terms, the first two areas of activity are primarily oriented toward increasing the prospects of individual Caribbean countries for selective delinkage and diversification within a regional South-South framework, while the last represents a means to acquire the assertive bargaining power necessary to renegotiate at least some of the terms of the West Indies' relationships with metropolitan centers of international power.

Recognize, however, that CARICOM's approach to integration did not, despite the organization's name, take the form of a conventional common market involving attempts to achieve production complementarity as well as freedom of movement for capital and labor. To the contrary, in order to shield the LDCs from the threat of having their local investment resources and their most skilled workers drained off by better economic opportunities in the larger members, restrictions were placed on the intraregional migration of both people and money. Indeed, aside from implementing a uniform external tariff and taking various steps to assure a more equitable distribution of the benefits created by greater developmental cooperation, CARICOM did not depart radically in its more technical aspects from the CARIFTA model. It was, in other words, basically a free trade association supplemented and bolstered by a customs union that provided some protection against attempts by outsiders to exploit the reduction of barriers to interisland commerce.

When it came to functional collaboration, however, CARICOM was much more ambitious than CARIFTA, launching joint ventures in health, air and sea transportation, and especially higher education. The University of the West Indies was established to serve the entire area with major campuses in Jamaica, Trinidad, and Barbados. Such initiatives were conceived with a dual purpose in mind. First, in a purely technocratic sense, it was hoped that they would create an infrastructure for future economic growth that, because it would be truly regional in scope, would help to ameliorate the size and viability problems that previously had always been a major factor behind the inability of the CARICOM countries to enjoy much significant long-term developmental progress. There was, however, a second and more nebulous dimension to such multilateralism, related to the concept popularized by functionalist theorists in the 1960s that socioeconomic cooperation could generate a spillover effect into the political arena, thereby laying the cornerstone for the emergence of a single unified state.[13] There is little if any evidence to indicate that CARICOM's functionalist projects have resulted in any markedly increased sentiment for, or movement toward, eventual political consolidation, but advocates of the hypothesis insist that it entails an extremely complex and protracted phenomenon that has not yet had enough time to play itself out.

Undoubtedly CARICOM's most innovative aspect was the commitment of its members to coordinate their foreign policies to the greatest possible degree; no other regional integration group in the Western Hemisphere had ever before been so audacious on such a wide range of issues. Over the years, says Anthony Bryan,

> the member states of CARICOM have successfully coordinated their policies at forums such as the ACP [Group], the UN, and the OAS [Organization of American States]. Similarly, there have been coordinated positions on specific issues, such as normalization of relations with Cuba, the Panama Canal, the Law of the Sea, Southern Africa, and the territorial claims facing Guyana and Belize [coming respectively from Venezuela and Guatemala]. They have also consulted on matters such as the Caribbean Basin Initiative and regional security.[14]

In reality, ideological differences or conflicting definitions of national interest have often made it difficult to attain consensus, one glaring example being the divergent stances assumed in 1983 concerning the necessity and legitimacy of Washington's decision to invade Grenada. But regardless of such problems, the formal incorporation of the principle of a united international front within the context of an association dedicated to promoting modernization on a broad regional scale clearly implied that CARICOM was intended to function as a mechanism for initiating and implementing collective bargaining between the West Indies and other actors on the global economic stage. In short, CARICOM was conceived at least in part as a means for the English-speaking Caribbean to acquire the political space and negotiating strength necessary to make the system state transition to controlled dependence. Thus the West Indians, who perhaps were sailing as blindly as Columbus almost five hundred years earlier when he made landfall there, prepared themselves to plunge into the murky waters of postdependency politics.

From an organizational perspective, there are actually two distinct institutional entities that operate under the CARICOM umbrella—the Common Market and the Community. Obviously those elements associated with the Common Market concentrate primarily on administering programs related to maintaining uniform external tariffs and enhancing free trade among the participants. The Community staff, on the other hand, is responsible for overseeing the political and functional facets of Caribbean integration (e.g., foreign policy coordination and provision of infrastructural services). Given this division of labor, it is the Community that provides postdependency leadership. The Common Market division can, of course, make a contribution to CARICOM's counterdependency efforts by facilitating diversification of a member's international relations and by assisting the efforts of the group as a whole to pursue selective delinkage from the metropolitan centers that have traditionally dominated the region. But it is the acquisition and wielding of assertive bargaining power that stand at the core of postdependency politics, and, since such activity falls under the purview of the Community because of its responsibility for foreign policy coordination, the Common Market's role in the process will be essentially supportive.

The CARICOM hierarchy established by the Treaty of Chaguaramas is schematically illustrated in Figure 3.1. The three main centers of authority and influence are the Heads of Government Conference (HGC), the Common Market Council of Ministers, and the Secretariat. Officially, ultimate decisionmaking power is vested in the HGC, where each participating country has one vote, and unanimity is required to pass recommendations (compliance here being voluntary) or binding resolutions. The HGC also holds the mandate for concluding treaties on CARICOM's behalf and for

Figure 3.1 Institutional Organization of the Caribbean Community

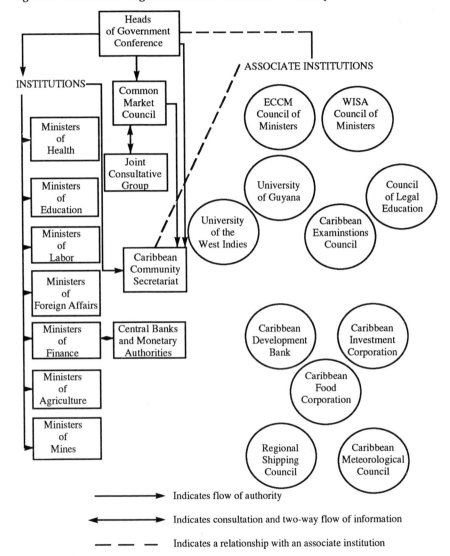

Indicates flow of authority

Indicates consultation and two-way flow of information

Indicates a relationship with an associate institution

(From W. Andrew Axline, *Caribbean Integration* [East Brunswick, NJ: Nichols Publishing Company, 1979], p. 79. Reprinted with permission.)

overseeing its relations with individual states or other international associations. In practice, however, the HGC often merely ratifies proposals that have been worked out within the Council of Ministers, whose membership provisions and voting procedures are practically identical to the HGC's. Although the Council meets as needed throughout the year, it inevitably convenes just prior to the annual CARICOM summit to finalize the details of the agenda items the prime ministers will consider (and usually accept without major modifications). Naturally, one factor complicating the work of both the HGC and the Council is that their members represent their governments and hence are very likely to give priority to national rather than CARICOM interests. Thus one must turn to the Secretariat to find the true nerve center of integrationist sentiment, since, like most other similar international bodies, its staff is prohibited from accepting instructions from any official at the national level and obligated to assure that their actions serve the Community rather than the parochial concerns of any of its members. According to Andrew Axline, the Secretariat

> has become the most dynamic element in the process of Caribbean integration. Drawing upon the expertise of the Secretariat, studies have been undertaken and policies designed which have provided the basis for inter-governmental negotiations and the adoption of integrative measures. The Secretariat, in fostering an ideology of integration, has provided a communications link among the various forces of the region, including intellectuals, the private sector and member governments. The Secretary-General himself has played an important role in negotiating compromises among member governments, often through personal contact and face-to-face discussions with heads of government. The Secretariat has also participated in missions to various countries in order to develop support for compromises on the adoption of regional policies. The Secretariat represents the vanguard of the Caribbean integration movement by attempting to build a regional consensus around measures which will constitute an integration scheme likely to contribute to the development of the region.[15]

Having finally created in CARICOM a vehicle with postdependency capabilities, the Caribbean states were now in a position to explore the potential for making the system state transition to controlled dependence by exercising the South-South option.

With the institutional machinery necessary to exploit the South-South option in place, operational issues naturally tended to move to the forefront. Two questions, which were not always openly articulated, emerged: Who would provide the leadership necessary to energize the process. And which of its specific facets would be emphasized? As had been the case in other instances, Guyana, Jamaica, and (to a somewhat lesser extent) Trinidad and Tobago quickly emerged as the CARICOM vanguard. These three countries—Guyana in particular—were attracted to the notion that the concept of joint management should be incorporated into the international economic system, which in effect represented a demand for the redistribution of decisionmaking and regulatory or administrative authority on a global scale. Implementing this scenario would, of course, almost inevitably entail complex North-South negotiations, which in turn implied that the LDCs would have to devote serious attention to interjecting a strong South-South dimension into their foreign policies in order to enhance their bargaining power. Functioning within this general framework, Guyana, Jamaica, and Trinidad and Tobago used their influence within CARICOM to promote greater attention to South-South politics.

Despite the apparent geographic and economic logic involved, the approach adopted by the English-speaking Caribbean and its vanguard states as they embarked on this South-South odyssey did not, at least initially, place a high premium on close collaboration with their Latin American neighbors. Instead, they chose to focus primarily on developing a broad Third World rather than a somewhat narrower hemispheric persona by closely identifying with the Afro-Asian countries and their concerns. This orientation led, in terms of specific policy outcomes, to a pattern of increasing activity on the part of CARICOM members in such major Third World advocacy or bargaining organizations as the Nonaligned Movement and the Group of 77.

The CARICOM States and the NAM:
The Quest for Greater South-South Cohesion

Founded in 1965 by twenty-five mostly Afro-Asian states (Cuba being the only charter member from the Western Hemisphere), the NAM tended to drift somewhat throughout the remainder of the decade. Little progress was made in developing an institutional infrastructure for organizing and coordinating ongoing activities between the summit conferences that were supposed to be held every three to four years. Moreover, the NAM was rather vague regarding its specific goals and functions; it was committed to the broad principles of peace and decolonization but did not establish itself as a dynamic force providing leadership in the struggle to attain these ends. Indeed, had it not been for the dedication of such respected individuals as Josip Broz (Tito) of Yugoslavia, Gamal Abdul Nasser of Egypt, and Sukarno of Indonesia in throwing their prestige behind the NAM, it in all likelihood would have dropped quietly out of the international picture for good.

The NAM's stock began to rise sharply in the early 1970s as it became a catalyst and rallying point for the growing concern of Third World states about their status and role in the global economy. Frustrated by their inability to make what they felt was sufficient progress toward modernization operating within the existing structures and rules, the LDCs became increasingly committed to a search for alternatives. Reflecting and building on such sentiments, the NAM soon became a center of agitation for the Third World's most ambitious dream—a new international economic order. The two landmark events in the genesis of the NIEO concept were the 1973 Nonaligned Summit held in Algiers and the Sixth Special Session of the UN General Assembly (April 9–May 2, 1974). According to Odette Jankowitsch and Karl Sauvant,

> the 1973 Algiers Summit, attended by the largest number of heads of state or government ever gathered in an international conference, encompassed the widest range of developmental objectives ever formulated at such a high political level. It is not so much the novelty of each individual proposal, but rather the integration of all proposals into one program, the intended orientation of this toward structural changes, and, above all, the level of endorsement which gives the Algiers Declaration and Action Programme its significance. It was recognized that the improvement of the situation of the developing countries is not only a technical matter but that this situation is embedded in an international environment whose mechanisms and structures are important determinants of the development process. The objective, therefore, became to change the international environment in such a way as to make it more responsive to the the needs of the developing countries.[16]

Following the Algiers Summit, the Sixth UN Special Session was convened at the behest of the Nonaligned Movement to study the problem of Third World development. It produced two major documents—the "Declaration on the Establishment of a New International Economic Order" and the "Programme of Action on the Establishment of a New International Economic Order."[17] Basically, then, the NAM was one of the major driving forces behind the effort to include the NIEO issue (which in many respects represented a response to the concern of the LDCs about dependency) on the North-South agenda.

The NAM's basic administrative configuration is shown in Figure 3.2. Its premier event is its summit conference, which normally occurs every three years and invariably attracts a long list of the Third World's most distinguished figures. Although major differences that need to be reconciled emerge sometimes at these meetings, the proceedings usually revolve around more ceremonial concerns such as announcing or reaffirming the consensus LDC position on various international issues and projecting the dynamic image necessary for the NAM to maintain a mobilizational capability.

The Movement's routine work occurs within the framework of the foreign ministers conferences and the NAM Coordinating Bureau. The foreign ministers of all the member countries meet prior to every summit to set the agenda and to finalize the details of the specific resolutions that will be considered (and usually adopted with few significant modifications) by

Figure 3.2 Organizational Structure of the Nonaligned Movement

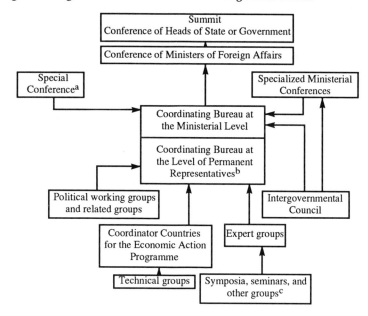

(From Odette Jankowitsch and Karl P. Sauvant, "The Initiating Role of The Nonaligned Countries," in Karl P. Sauvant, ed., *Changing Priorities on the International Agenda: The New International Economic Order* [New York: Pergamon Press, 1982], p. 50.)

[a]The first Special Conference, Cairo 1962, took place before the establishment of the Bureau.

[b]The Coordinating Bureau at the Level of Permanent Representatives also functions as the preparatory committee for summits, foreign minister conferences, and meetings of the Bureau at the ministerial level.

[c]If no competent expert group exists, these meetings may report to any other body of the Nonaligned Movement.

the nonaligned leaders. Other ministerial conclaves are held as needed to oversee the implementation of the organization's programs. The Coordinating Bureau (whose participants are chosen to serve three-year terms on the basis of a geographical formula whereby approximately 48 percent of the seats are allocated to Africa, 32 percent to Asia, 16 percent to Latin America, and 4 percent to Europe) in effect functions as the administrative secretariat for the NAM, especially at the level of the permanent representatives. One of the Bureau's most important duties is to monitor the work of those nations that are coordinating various aspects of the Movement's Economic Action Programme (which grew out of the 1972 foreign ministers' session in Guyana and essentially seeks to stimulate greater cooperation among LDCs in a wide variety of functional areas).[18] The activities of these supervisory groups, generally composed of three to eight members led by one who is designated the principal coordinator, can cover a broad spectrum ranging from such mundane pursuits as circulating technical reports to orchestrating sprawling interregional programs. Admittedly, this system for facilitating developmental collaboration has not consistently produced dramatic results. It has, nevertheless, become a permanent fixture of the Nonaligned Movement, symbolizing the Third World commitment to exploring the South-South option as a means to diversify economic relations and to help create an environment wherein LDCs can acquire the bargaining power required to attain and sustain effective sovereignty within a context of controlled dependence and ongoing postdependency politics.

Generally there was little CARICOM participation in the NAM during the 1960s and most of the 1970s (see Table 3.1). Instead, most of the Anglophone countries were preoccupied at the time with gaining independence or organizing CARIFTA and CARICOM as mechanisms for

Table 3.1 The CARICOM Contingent in the Nonaligned Movement

	Full Members	Permanent Observers
Belgrade Summit, 1961	0	0
Cairo Summit, 1964	0	Jamaica Trinidad and Tobago
Lusaka Summit, 1970	Guyana Jamaica Trinidad and Tobago	Barbados
Colombo Summit, 1976[a]	Guyana Jamaica Trinidad and Tobago	Barbados Grenada
Havana Summit, 1979[a]	Grenada Guyana Jamaica Trinidad and Tobago	Barbados Dominica St. Lucia
New Delhi Summit, 1983	Bahamas Barbados Belize Grenada Guyana Jamaica St. Lucia Trinidad and Tobago	Antigua and Barbuda Dominica

Sources: Odette Jankowitsch and Karl P. Sauvant, "The Initiating Role of the Nonaligned Countries," in Karl P. Sauvant, ed., *Changing Priorities on the International Agenda: The New International Economic Order* (New York: Pergamon Press, 1981), pp. 44–48; *Two Decades of Nonalignment* (New Delhi: Ministry of External Affairs, 1983), p. 401; and Richard L. Jackson, *The Nonaligned, the U.N., and the Superpowers* (New York: Praeger Publishers, 1983), pp. 279–282.
[a]Belize was given special consultive status.

intra-Caribbean cooperation. This emphasis on more local concerns is, of course, understandable and indeed not particularly unusual; the natural tendency for most LDCs is not to get heavily involved in the larger arenas of South-South politics until they have resolved the more immediate problems of regional cohesion. This approach is particularly appropriate for small states such as those in the West Indies, for they must always be sensitive to the fact that their size and resource limitations put them in a potentially disadvantageous position when they try to operate as individual actors on the world stage. Thus most CARICOM countries were inclined to concentrate first on establishing their own Caribbean associations, which could then be utilized as vehicles for expanding their spheres of international activity. The major exceptions to this rule were, of course, Guyana and Jamaica, whose penchant for plunging into the mainstream of nonaligned affairs was symptomatic of the vanguard role they sought to play both within the NAM and in broadening the South-South horizons of the West Indian community.

Guyana quickly assumed a very high profile in the Nonaligned Movement. For example, shortly after being admitted in 1969, it secured a seat on the committee that later evolved into the NAM's Coordinating Bureau. The Bureau is one of the organization's main nerve centers, and by maintaining its seat there over the years, Guyana has been in a good position to exercise influence. Guyana first made its presence felt in a major way when it was selected to host the August 1972 Foreign Ministers Conference. As Lloyd Searwar notes,

> several students of the Movement have held that this conference led to its revitalization and to an important addition to its Agendas, namely, the programme of collective self-reliance as outlined in the Georgetown Action Programme of Economic Co-operation among Nonaligned and other Developing Countries (ECDC). This was, in fact, the first programme of ECDC adopted by the developing world. It is indisputable that the hosting of this conference earned Guyana a major leadership role [in the NAM].[19]

This newfound status was evidenced by the fact that Guyana was appointed at the Georgetown conference to serve as the principal coordinator country in the crucial area of trade, transport, and industry. In this capacity, it quickly emerged as a leading advocate of South-South economic cooperation not only within the NAM, but also in other major international fora such as the Group of 77. Subsequently Guyana was also appointed to serve on the Movement's Working Groups at the United Nations dealing with the Solidarity Fund for the Reconstruction of Vietnam and Laos; Southern Africa; the Solidarity Fund for the Liberation of Southern Africa; Cyprus; and Non-Interference in the Internal Affairs of States. The members of these groups sponsor resolutions, organize support for them, coordinate speakers, and generally serve as floor managers seeking to assure that the

United Nations adopts positions consistent with those of the Nonaligned Movement.

Jamaica joined the NAM in 1968, but initially its enthusiasm fell far short of Guyana's. For example, while Georgetown was engrossed in its campaign to establish its nonaligned leadership credentials, Kingston displayed its indifference to such pursuits by generally dispatching rather low-level representatives to NAM meetings and often being reluctant to take stances it felt were incompatible with its close ties to the United States. In 1972, however, this situation changed dramatically when Michael Manley assumed power determined to make Jamaica's presence felt in Third World circles. Indeed Manley soon became associated with the NAM's Cuban-led radical wing and emerged as a prominent advocate of the NIEO at the 1973 Nonaligned Summit in Algiers,[20] thus contributing to what many observers felt was a major shift by the organization toward a much more assertive and in some respects confrontational posture toward the North on developmentally related issues. Such moves on Manley's part derived from a commitment to South-South postdependency politics involving, according to Winston Langley, a

> strategy [that] was twofold: gain increased power needed to deal with industrial states by forming regional groupings and, in a broader thrust, pursue the development of "a common economic policy" among Third World states. In other words, the power Jamaica needs to improve its bargaining positon versus developed states can, in part, be found through regional ties with the Caribbean; and the power of the latter can, in turn, be enhanced by a broader collaboration with the rest of the Third World.[21]

Accordingly, Kingston became a coordinator for the NAM's ECDC Action Programme with regard to the Role of Women in Development as well as Tourism and also participated in two of its UN Working Groups (Southern Africa and United Nations Affairs). During the 1980s, of course, Jamaica's attachment to the NAM once again waned as the Seaga government almost completely reversed Kingston's foreign policy orientations and transformed the island into one of the Reagan administration's most trustworthy Caribbean allies.

A major influx of Caribbean–Latin American states into the NAM occurred in the late 1970s and early 1980s; ten of the seventeen hemispheric nations holding full membership at the time of the 1983 New Delhi Summit had joined sometime during the 1979–1983 period,[22] with all the CARICOM countries except Montserrat (which was not independent and therefore not eligible to hold a seat), St. Vincent and the Grenadines, and St. Kitts–Nevis involved as regular participants or permanent observers (see Table 3.1). There were, however, some alterations in the activist complexion of the Caribbean contingent. Jamaica, having in effect subordinated the South-

South dimension to the Singapore option after Edward Seaga won the 1980 general elections, was no longer interested in playing a leading role in the struggle for an NIEO or practically any other cause the island had embraced under Manley's leadership. Instead, the Seaga regime was content to become a foot soldier in the moderate-conservative bloc that was seeking to undermine the influence Cuba and other radicals had acquired in the Movement.[23] On the other hand, while Kingston was in the process of abandoning the nonaligned vanguard, Grenada was making a concerted effort to enter it. Indeed, until it disintegrated in October 1983 under the dual pressures of internal factionalism and the U.S.–orchestrated invasion, Maurice Bishop's New Jewel government was probably more attracted than any of its CARICOM colleagues to following a South-South strategy within the NAM.

The remainder of the 1980s saw Guyana once again emerging as the most active CARICOM state in the NAM as a result of such initiatives as its involvement in the growing debate over the controversial issue of a new world information order (NWIO). Indeed it was elected vice-chairman of the First Conference of Nonaligned Information Ministers, which met in Djakarta, Indonesia, for five days in January 1984 to begin formulating a detailed Third World position on various NWIO questions.[24] The other members of the West Indian delegation remained committed in principle to the organization, but by and large none of them as individuals carved out a special niche for itself in it nor did the CARICOM group function collectively as a highly assertive regional lobby. This relative quiescence notwithstanding, the NAM has had and continues to have significant implications for CARICOM counterdependency politics.

If NAM membership is evaluated in a purely instrumental post-dependency light that stresses such material benefits as increased South-South trade or major concessions attained in North-South negotiations, there clearly is reason for one to be skeptical about its utility. Such an approach fails, however, to appreciate that there is a crucial psychological dimension of the nonaligned equation. Unfortunately, many small countries such as those in the West Indies tend to be plagued with identity problems. Too often they are seen, both by outsiders and even by some of their own people, as destined by fate to live in the hegemonic shadow of a larger, more powerful neighbor. NAM affiliation can, however, serve as an antidote to such perceptions, thereby providing a means for the West Indies to go beyond the unflattering stereotype wherein a Caribbean identity is equated with "backyard status" and begin to establish their political personalities in much broader Third World terms. Such a conceptualization represents a critical subjective step that needs to be taken before more substantive counterdependency measures can be launched. In effect, then, NAM affiliation represents a declaration of independence or assertiveness that serves notice that countries such as the CARICOM states have redefined their international role to include a significant South-South component and are to be taken seriously as players in postdependency politics by other LDCs as well as by the metropolitan powers. Thus, just as admission to the United Nations tends to be symbolic of formal sovereignty for Third World states, so also is entry into the Nonaligned Movement seen as a watershed signifying the high priority given to utilizing the South-South option to help achieve full effective sovereignty.

While it may be tempting to dismiss such aspects of NAM membership as so ethereal as to be functionally meaningless with regard to solving the concrete developmental problems at the core of postdependency politics, this critique is in many respects a straw man exercise, since the Movement has for the most part been oriented in other directions. Specifically, the NAM has always emphasized promoting Third World unity on matters of general principle and policy; it does not normally seek to serve as the actual means for operationalizing them. Thus CARICOM's involvement in the Movement should not be seen mainly as an attempt to procure immediate, material rewards, but rather as indicative of a commitment to enhancing South-South unity. The key agenda items, in other words, do not entail arranging the specific modalities of trade diversification or exercising bargaining power within the context of highly technical North-South negotiations, but rather focus on the task of facilitating Third World consensus and cohesion on postdependency issues, which will then be pursued through other channels, particularly the G-77. This division of labor, says Leelananda de Silva, means that the NAM is

> primarily concerned with the organization of a countervailing power within the Third World and the creation of conditions for organic unity within it, and the [G-77] is concerned more with the utilization of this strength and power in the external dimension of negotiations with the North, especially within UNCTAD, and in the improvement of international markets for trade in commodities, capital, technology, labour, and so on.[25]

In this sense, therefore, the Nonaligned Movement represents the general staff, while the G-77 constitutes the front-line troops of the Third World's South-South counterdependency campaign.

The CARICOM States and the Group of 77

The Group of 77, which is a misnomer since its ranks had already grown to approximately 125 nations by the early 1980s, emerged out of the first UNCTAD meeting in 1964. Conceived originally as a forum wherein the LDCs could develop a united front for the North-South economic negotiations occurring within the UNCTAD framework, the G-77 later expanded its sphere of action to include the United Nations Industrial Development Organization (UNIDO), the World Bank and International Monetary Fund, and the UN headquarters operations in New York.

Rather than creating a single directorate to oversee and coordinate the organization's activities in these four main theaters, the G-77 opted for a much more decentralized approach. For example, in contrast to the NAM, the G-77 has no recognized leader; no country or individual is designated as its international representative nor is there anybody comparable to the NAM's Coordinating Bureau to serve as the functional equivalent of a secretariat for the association as a whole. Instead, the G-77 had by the early 1980s established basically autonomous administrative and operational structures for each of its four primary areas of concern (see Figure 3.3). In each realm, the Ministerial Meeting represents the formal locus of power and authority. Such assemblies do not take place on a regular schedule (e.g., annually or quarterly), but rather are convened as needed, the most common reason being to finalize an LDC bargaining package for a major upcoming round of international economic talks. The responsibility for conducting business between ministerial meetings rests with coordinator countries, the appointments generally rotating on an annual basis among the African, Asian, and Latin American contingents.

While the diffuseness and fluidity that tend to characterize the G-77's upper echelons may be advantageous in the sense that they inject flexibility into its organizational personality, these are not traits likely to assure that the routine technocratic tasks required to develop sophisticated program or negotiating proposals will be done systematically. The various working groups operating at the grass-roots level thus become vital, for they constitute the true nerve centers wherein much of the G-77's substantive work is actually carried out. Traditionally, the UNCTAD division has had permanent working groups,[26] while elsewhere they have usually been created on an ad hoc basis to deal with specific short-term problems. Countries generally acquire a seat in a working group simply by volunteering their services, the one caveat to open membership being that an effort is made to guarantee that Africa, Asia, and Latin America are equally represented.

The G-77 has displayed an approach to postdependency politics that has in many respects been quite similar to the paradigm outlined in Chapter 2. Both scenarios stress diversification and assertive (collective) bargaining. The G-77 formulation has, however, tended to reverse these priorities, viewing increased South-South economic collaboration as a backup plan that can and should be activated if the prospects for fruitful North-South dialog seem dim.

Certainly one of the G-77's most ambitious forays into North-South bargaining was the Paris Conference on International Economic Cooperation (CIEC), which involved a series of sessions over an eighteen-month period

Figure 3.3 **Organizational Structure of the Group of 77 (1981)**

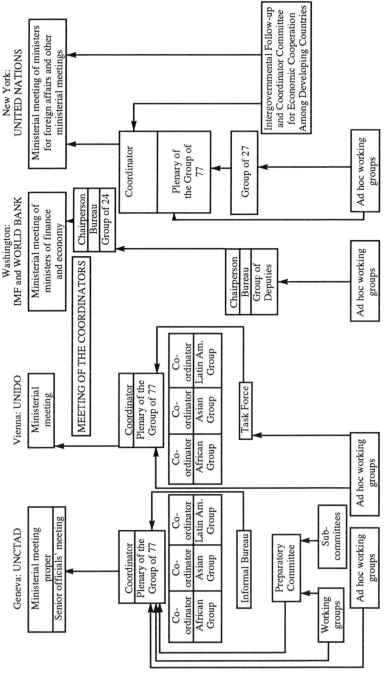

(From Karl P. Sauvant, "Organizational Infrastructure for Self-Reliance: The Non-Aligned Countries and the Group of 77," in Breda Pavlic et al., eds., *The Challenges of South-South Cooperation* [Boulder, CO: Westview Press, 1983], p. 55. Reprinted with permission.)

stretching from January 1976 to June 1977. Nineteen Third World countries represented the G-77, while the northern delegation had eight participants.[27] The four main items on the negotiating agenda were energy, raw materials, development, and financial affairs, with the substantive discussions proceeding simultaneously in four separate commissions (or committees) where in each case an LDC and an industrialized nation cochaired.[28] Within this format, says Robert Mortimer,

> the prompt consolidation of the Group of 19 and its explicit association with the Group of 77 established the political ground rules of the Paris Conference. The developing states were committed to a bloc strategy and insisted upon the integration of CIEC into the total environment of North-South politics. This strategy was designed to maintain the cohesion of the larger coalition as the more important long-term instrument. These early moves made it evident that the success of the conference depended upon the satisfaction of the major grievances of the developing world.[29]

But despite agreements on some important initiatives, such as the establishment of a special billion-dollar fund to aid the most destitute Third World nations, the G-77 negotiators were generally disappointed with the CIEC because they felt that no meaningful progress was made toward the achievement of a new, more equitable global order. In effect, then, they had failed to transform their bargaining power into structural power.

Another highly publicized North-South encounter was the summit held in Cancún, Mexico, in October 1981. Thirteen G-77 members accepted invitations to participate, hoping that they would be able to persuade the new Reagan administration to make a firm commitment to reopen the dialog on NIEO questions. The White House, however, proved to be more interested in photo opportunities than substantive discussions. Indeed, prior to the conference Washington had preconditioned its attendance on assurances that no formal negotiations would occur, no concrete accords would be reached, and no final, official communiqués would be issued.[30] Whatever collective bargaining power the Third World nations might have had was meaningless under such circumstances, for the Reagan restrictions assured that it could not be utilized. It was, therefore, hardly surprising that nothing significant transpired; speeches were made, long-established positions were reiterated, optimism about future progress was expressed, and no problems were solved.

Such frustrating experiences engendered some sentiment in the G-77 to abandon the negotiating track and concentrate almost solely on promoting collective self-reliance. The majority, however, were not willing to risk the radical delinking of their ties with the North that this scenario implied. Instead, they tended to stress the less drastic concept of ECDC as a means to alleviate somewhat the Third World's suffering during what they hoped would not be too long a process of structural transformation of the global economy leading eventually to a system characterized by balanced interdependence. Such a stance is consistent with the G-77's tradition of encouraging ECDC. The first major move in this direction took place at a 1976 ministerial meeting in Manila where the ECDC principle was incorporated into the organization's permanent agenda. Subsequently the special Intergovernmental Follow-Up and Coordination Committee, along with a rather elaborate support structure (see Figure 3.4), was established as part of a detailed action program adopted at the G-77's May 1981 Conference on Economic Cooperation Among Developing Countries held in Caracas, Venezuela. This follow-up committee eventually overshadowed its companion UNCTAD working group as the central clearinghouse for G-77 ECDC activity.

Perhaps because the G-77, in contrast to the NAM, was perceived by most CARICOM states as being less politicized and more oriented toward coming directly to grips with concrete developmental problems, they were less hesitant to join its ranks. Consequently the West Indian states tended to become participants shortly after achieving independence, with Jamaica and

Figure 3.4 Organizational Structure of the Group of 77 Regarding Economic Cooperation Among Developing Countries, December 1981 (as agreed at the High-Level Conference on Economic Co-operation Among Developing Countries, Caracas, May 13–19, 1981)

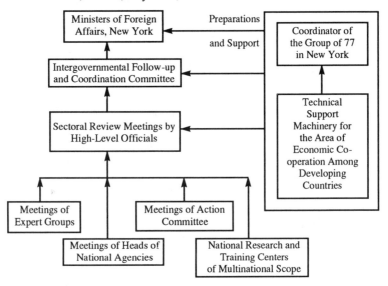

(From Karl P. Sauvant, "Organizational Infrastructure for Self-Reliance: The Non-Aligned Countries and the Group of 77," in *The Challenges of South-South Cooperation* [Boulder, CO: Westview Press, 1983], p. 64. Reprinted with permission.)

Trinidad and Tobago being the two charter members from the region. Initially Kingston surged to the CARICOM forefront in assuming a vanguard role within the G-77, with Trinidad and Tobago and Guyana also maintaining fairly high profiles.

Jamaica's rapid emergence as one of the most active CARICOM countries in the G-77 can to some extent be illustrated by comparing its participation in the organization's crucial UNCTAD working groups to that of other West Indian nations during the late 1970s and early 1980s (see Table 3.2). It could be argued, however, that to be involved in working groups where membership is basically a matter of self-selection hardly indicates any kind of vanguard status within the organization. If the affiliations shown in Table 3.2 represented the sum total of Kingston's activities, such a contention might have some merit. But Kingston's stature must be seen in qualitative and reputational as well as purely quantitative terms, in which case its assignment to represent the Third World in such potentially important North-South negotiations as the CIEC becomes more consequential as a measure of the G-77's esteem.

Table 3.2 CARICOM Membership in G-77 UNCTAD Working Groups (September 1981)

Jamaica	Trinidad and Tobago	Others
Commodities and the Common Fund	Commodities and the Common Fund	(None)
Economic Cooperation Among LDCs	Institutional Questions	
Monetary/Financial Issues	Multilateral Trade Negotiations	
Multilateral Trade Negotiations	Restrictive Business Practices	
Technology Transfers	Shipping	
International Development Strategy		

In recognition of the Manley government's strong commitment to South-South politics and the NIEO concept, Jamaica was chosen as one of the nineteen Third World countries that would negotiate on the G-77's behalf with the bloc of western industrialized nations at the Paris Conference on International Economic Cooperation that began in January 1976. Kingston was, in a sense, not only representing the Caribbean in Paris, but also the

Third World's ministates in general, since it was the smallest LDC (in terms of both population and geographic size) at the meeting. Certainly it does not appear, however, that its prestige and influence were adversely affected by its lack of the traditional attributes of power; for example, Jamaica also played a major role in the fourth UNCTAD meeting (May 1976 in Nairobi), which in turn had a significant impact on the CIEC proceedings that had just gotten under way. The UNCTAD meeting provided an opportunity for the G-77 to refine and expand the negotiating agenda it would be pursuing in Paris. Jamaica was elected the coordinating country for UNCTAD IV, which in effect placed it at the very epicenter of the complex North-South dialog then in progress.

But Jamaica certainly was not the only CARICOM activist in the G-77 during this crucial period, for both Guyana and Trinidad and Tobago were also making their presence felt. At the UNCTAD IV conference, notes Denis Benn, Georgetown, given its already solid track record of

> active involvement in the negotiation of economic issues in the United Nations and other international fora, was . . . elected Vice-Chairman of Negotiating Group IV, which dealt with the problems of the least developed countries, landlocked and island developing countries. It also chaired the Drafting Group appointed by the Conference on Economic Cooperation Among Developing Countries. In addition, Trinidad and Tobago was appointed spokesman of the Group of Seventy-Seven on the problems of island developing countries—an agenda item in which the Caribbean countries, Trinidad and Tobago in particular, had taken a special interest in view of their insular character.[31]

Guyana was also prominent at the G-77 ministerial meeting that convened in Tanzania (January 1979) to prepare for the upcoming UNCTAD V conference in Manila (May 1979), having been successfully nominated by the Latin American contingent to serve as the chair of Negotiating Group Two (whose purview encompassed such issues as international trade, manufacturing, technology transfers, and shipping). Concurrent with all these high-visibility ventures, Trinidad and Tobago continued to do yeoman's duty in the trenches of the G-77's permanent UNCTAD working groups. This pattern of CARICOM activism within the G-77 framework continued into the early 1980s, as epitomized by the fact that Forbes Burnham of Guyana was one of the fourteen Third World leaders invited to attend the highly touted, but ultimately ill-fated 1981 North-South summit conference in Cancún.[32]

In general, then, it appears that CARICOM's interests have been rather well represented in most of the major postdependency initiatives undertaken by the G-77, even though only a handful of West Indian states have in many instances been directly involved. The possibility that such limited participation might severely restrict the G-77's exposure to all the various shades of Caribbean opinion that may exist regarding any particular issue is counterbalanced by the fact that foreign policy coordination is one of CARICOM's core principles. That being so, even though efforts to operationalize the concept have not always been completely successful, a mechanism for consultation and collaboration has been instituted to maximize the probability that the individual CARICOM nations that are significant players in G-77 activities will serve as transmission belts for the concerns of the West Indian community as a whole. Thus, even if CARICOM as an organizational entity, or a majority of its members, is not a key actor in international negotiations, the structural dynamics of the Caribbean–G-77 relationship are such that the latter can in effect function as the former's collective bargaining agent. CARICOM thereby acquires, indirectly but nevertheless substantively, postdependency bargaining power at the very highest global level of North-South politics.

Forging a Hemispheric Link:
CARICOM'S Evolving Multilateral Ties with Latin America

Both the CARICOM and mainland Hispanic communities were as a whole sluggish in beginning to explore the potential benefits that might result from promoting interregional cooperation and solidarity. Instead, to the extent that there was any significant intercourse in the late 1960s and early 1970s, it tended to occur at the bilateral rather than the multilateral level, with Venezuela and Mexico being the key actors on the Latin side. Caracas, for example, capitalizing on the opportunities presented by the precipitous rise in petroleum prices during the early 1970s to enhance its influence in the Caribbean Basin, began to offer various kinds of aid to some of the CARICOM states to offset the hardships created by the greatly inflated prices they now had to pay to cover their oil imports. Credit lines, often quite generous, were extended to Barbados, Guyana, and Jamaica while negotiations were undertaken with other islands aimed at providing other forms of economic or technical assistance. The personal friendship between Michael Manley and Carlos Andrés Pérez translated into unusually strong Jamaican-Venezuelan relations, as illustrated by Pérez's announcement during an April 1975 visit that Caracas would make arrangements to sell oil to Kingston below market rates as well as commit itself to long-term contracts to purchase Jamaican bauxite. Mexico, although traditionally more attracted to Central America than the CARICOM region, also launched some bilateral Caribbean initiatives during this period, perhaps the most controversial being a 1974 joint-venture agreement with Jamaica calling for the construction and operation of aluminum plants in both countries. Trinidad and Tobago's Eric Williams was infuriated by this deal, insisting that it was incompatible with a previously proposed Trinidadian-Jamaican-Guyanese project. This dispute as well as other considerations led Mexico, in 1978, to disavow any further interest.[33] Such linkages, however, were more the exception than the rule; in general, there was not at this point any great enthusiasm for the concept of West Indian–Latin American rapprochement, especially at the macroregional level.

Part, if not much, of this hesitancy can be attributed to cultural-historical factors. In particular, the Latins were suspicious of the fact that, while the CARICOM nations had repudiated western imperialism in terms of achieving statehood, they continued to maintain very close relations with London and enthusiastically embraced the British parliamentary system of government. Such attitudes were seen by many Hispanics as evidence that the Anglophone countries had not made a complete break with their colonial past and therefore could not be trusted as partners, since they really were not fully independent (in either a psychological or behavioral sense). In 1969, for example, Jamaica's application to join the OAS was initially vetoed by Bolivia on the grounds that Kingston had not, despite having achieved independence in 1962, broken all of its colonial ties with England. The marked difference in political cultures also constituted a barrier to mutual understanding and empathy. The West Indians were, whether deliberately or not, frequently somewhat contemptuous of the Latins' seeming inability or unwillingness to jettison their authoritarian and dictatorial traditions. The Hispanics, on the other hand, were often just as prone to view CARICOM's Westminster systems as alien imports that had little relevance to the needs and conditions of developing societies in the Western Hemisphere. The negative perceptions on both sides generated by such cognitive filters were, along with substantive policy differences, a major consideration impeding the emergence of more cooperative West Indian–Latin American ties.

Gradually, however, the two regions began to display a much greater interest in working together within a multilateral context. The first serious overtures to Latin America from the West Indian camp were, says Anthony Bryan,

> made by the government of Trinidad and Tobago, which had long-standing political and cultural ties with neighboring Venezuela. First came a firm pledge from Trinidad in 1967 to join the Latin American states in their increased drive for economic integration; then the pursuit of government and private sector cooperation through Trinidad/Venezuelan Mixed Commissions in 1967 and 1968. These initiatives were complemented by Trinidad's admission to the Organization of American States (OAS) in 1967. In their search for new economic links to take the place of their traditional colonial ties, other West Indian nations soon followed suit.[34]

Certainly one dramatic indication that the CARICOM community was beginning to endorse the concept of incorporating a vigorous Latin American dimension into its larger South-South agenda was the growing willingness of its members to emulate Port of Spain in joining the OAS. Barbados likewise became a member in 1967, followed by Jamaica (1969), Grenada (1975), and Dominica as well as St. Lucia in 1979. Subsequently the other CARICOM states also affiliated, except Guyana and Belize, which were ineligible under OAS criteria because of their unresolved border disputes with countries that had already been admitted (i.e., Venezuela and Guatemala respectively),[35] and Montserrat, which is excluded since it is still technically British territory. This convergence did not, of course, always flow smoothly, yet by the mid-1970s the tides were clearly running in favor of expanded collaboration in the struggle against underdevelopment and in the surge to make the transition to controlled dependence.

A major move in this direction came with the establishment in August 1975 of SELA, which at one level was designed to furnish a mechanism for coordinating its members' positions on international developmental issues and to facilitate the formation of more issue-specific functional bodies. But beyond these practical concerns was the commitment to a South-South strategy on the psychological and political plane, which SELA demanded and which was symbolized by the emphasis that its main proponents—Mexico and Venezuela—put on the idea that the United States had to be explicitly barred from participation, since the organization was designed first and foremost to serve and promote the common interests of the hemisphere's developing countries. This exclusion served notice that SELA was not to be viewed from a traditional pan-American perspective (which implied a role for the United States), but rather was assuming an unequivocally Third World identity. In postdependency terms, then, SELA was from the very beginning conceived as a vehicle for the Latin American–Caribbean nations to acquire greater political space through systematic intrahemispheric diversification and ultimately to exercise assertive collective bargaining power in their dealings with the industrialized North. SELA's strongest CARICOM supporters were Guyana and Jamaica, with Barbados, Grenada, and Trinidad and Tobago also becoming members.

The growing recognition of the potential benefits involved in developing a solid Latin connection was reaffirmed by the members of the Caribbean Committee of Development and Cooperation, which was established at the behest of all the major Hispanic and English-speaking islands in November 1975 as an affiliate of the United Nations' ECLA, when they included in the Committee's constitution a statement declaring their determination to "further a more complete identification of the positions and interests of the Caribbean countries with the rest of Latin America, recognizing [SELA] as the proper framework, on the level of the region as a whole, for exercising cooperation, consultation, and coordination among the member countries."[36]

Two concrete manifestations of such sentiments were the creation of the Caribbean Multinational Shipping Company (NAMUCAR) and the efforts to revitalize the Latin American Energy Organization (OLADE).

NAMUCAR was founded in December 1975, the charter members being Mexico, Venezuela, Cuba, Jamaica, and Costa Rica. Its basic purpose, of course, was to reduce the transportation costs of trade within the Caribbean Basin in particular and the Western Hemisphere in general by functioning in such a manner as to assure that the developmental interests of its participants were accorded priority equal to, if not greater than, the exigencies of profit making. In the case of OLADE, which had been rather quiescent following its creation in 1973, the impetus for the desire to strengthen it came mainly from the havoc that skyrocketing oil prices were wreaking on the trade balances of many hemispheric states, particularly the poorer ones. Consequently, with Mexico and Venezuela in the lead, initiatives were launched in September 1975 that sought to utilize OLADE as the vehicle for arriving at agreements on such energy-related issues as production enhancement, market development, resource exchanges, and financing, the ultimate goal being to move the Latin American–Caribbean community as close to self-sufficiency as possible. Although neither NAMUCAR nor OLADE proved to be as effective as had been hoped, for both were plagued with political dissension that tended to paralyze them, they nevertheless represented the vanguard in an ongoing process of Caribbean–Latin American experimentation in South-South economic cooperation.

Multilateral political and diplomatic cooperation has not developed as vigorously as has been the case in the economic realm; certainly the CARICOM states have not, for example, assumed any official obligation (either individually or collectively) to coordinate their foreign policies with their Hispanic neighbors. Thus, once again, the spillover effect predicted by classical functionalist theory has not materialized to any highly significant extent. Informally, however, there has been some progress, as illustrated by the fact that there has, according to Jacqueline Braveboy-Wagner, generally been a pattern of increased voting convergence between the CARICOM and Latin American contingents in the United Nations.[37] Moreover, with regard to the crisis in Central America that dominated the hemispheric agenda throughout most of the 1980s, the CARICOM nations generally sided with the major Hispanic countries in supporting the Contadora process and related "Latin initiatives" as the preferred mechanisms for handling the problem.

While progress has clearly occurred on a number of important fronts, the evolving CARICOM–Latin American connection must be characterized as still somewhat fragile. Suspicion and distrust persist; in particular, each party appears to have reservations about the other's credentials as a reliable political partner. Thus the Hispanics continue, says Anthony Bryan, to misinterpret the special relationship which exists between Europe and the Caribbean [and which involves] special trading relationships, e.g. Lomé, the maintenance of the Westminster political system in many islands, membership in the Commonwealth of Nations, and, needless to say, the fact that some Caribbean territories are yet to achieve independence. The Caribbean is therefore viewed as not only dependent on external powers but perhaps vulnerable to manipulation against the interests of Latin American states.[38]

Both the Falkland Islands/Malvinas war, wherein most CARICOM states were reluctant to wholeheartedly support Argentina, and the invasion of Grenada rekindled Hispanic doubts about how serious the West Indians really were about distancing themselves from the North and embracing Third World causes. The Caribbean countries, on the other hand, thought that the Latins were being insensitive and unreasonable, especially in the Falklands/Malvinas case, in which CARICOM members felt that they could hardly be expected to accept the use of force to settle hemispheric territorial disputes when two of their own—Guyana and Belize—were involved in such controversies with much more powerful Hispanic neighbors.

In general, the West Indians have not been hesitant to accuse the Latins of being arrogant and perhaps even racist in their attitudes toward their small Caribbean colleagues, a common catalyst for such sentiments being reluctance on the Hispanics' part to support CARICOM candidates for high offices in hemispheric or global organizations. Such a confrontation erupted in 1984 when Valarie McComie of Barbados, who had been active in OAS affairs since 1967 and had been serving as the organization's assistant secretary-general for approximately four years, was stymied in his bid to be elected secretary-general by Latin opposition. A similar incident occurred in 1988 when the Latin American contingent successfully countered the attempt of Dame Nita Barrow, Barbados' ambassador to the United Nations, to become president of the General Assembly by putting forward their own candidate (Dante Caputo, Argentina's foreign minister), thereby prompting Barbados' foreign minister to warn that if "some Latin countries believe that we in the Caribbean must settle for consolation prizes and shouldn't be allowed to get the plums of the system, that attitude must change."[39] Yet despite such residual handicaps, both the West Indians and the Latin Americans seem for the most part to be dedicated to advancing cooperation as part of the larger South-South dimension of their foreign policies.[40]

The South-South Option Bears Fruit:
CARICOM and the Lomé Conventions, 1975–1990

When we operate within a postdependency paradigm, the Lomé process emerges as the most significant and ambitious foray the CARICOM states (working in concert with a large group of African and Pacific LDCs) have undertaken in terms of trying to wield assertive bargaining power within a context of broad multilateral North-South negotiations. Certainly the West Indians, while undoubtedly engaging in a bit of political hyperbole, were initially rather effusive in their optimism about the potential benefits involved, hailing them as "revolutionary," "a turning point in history," and the equivalent of "a new Marshall Plan." Although reality later tempered such rhetoric by transforming some expectations into frustrations (which is perhaps inevitable in any set of long-term negotiations), the Lomé scenario nevertheless is a unique and fascinating experiment in North-South collective bargaining.

The roots of the first Lomé Convention (1975) can be traced to England's decision in the late 1960s to join the EC. Its pending entry sent shock waves through the Caribbean, raising fears that the privileged ties London had accorded to its former colonies would be totally jettisoned. West Indian sugar growers were particularly alarmed, for they recognized that the EC's Common Agricultural Policy would prohibit England from continuing to provide them the guaranteed market access they enjoyed under existing arrangements. Such trepidation was not limited to the Caribbean, but instead touched practically all Third World members of the British Commonwealth. Consequently, when given the opportunity under the provisions of the January 1972 Treaty of Accession, which ushered London into the EC, to establish an institutionalized association with the entire community, the Caribbean and other developing Commonwealth nations formed the ACP (Africa/Caribbean/Pacific) Group to function as their collective bargaining agent.

With the CARICOM states in the vanguard, ACP membership was expanded to include the former colonies of other European powers (especially France), and the forty-six participating governments then entered into negotiations in pursuit of a comprehensive new relationship with the EC. The result was the 1975 Lomé (I) Convention, which has subsequently been renegotiated every five years (i.e., Lomé II, 1980; III, 1985; and IV, 1990). The primary analytical emphasis here focuses on Lomé I–III, since they were at the time of writing the only complete versions in the sense that not only have they been ratified, but also their provisions have been implemented and thus they have a well-established performance record that can be evaluated.

Lomé I was not totally unprecedented, for the EC had already extended preferential treatment to some former European colonies before the Commonwealth issue was raised in connection with Britain's application for membership. The 1963 Yaounde accords, for instance, provided special associated status for eighteen African states (mostly former French territories).[41] Similar provisions were made for Kenya, Tanzania, and Uganda under the 1968 Arusha Convention. Thus, in certain respects, Lomé I represented a consolidation of a number of existing European–Third World agreements.

The negotiations culminating in the first Lomé treaty began in July 1973. Although London's EC membership was the main catalyst for the process, particularly from the ACP perspective, there were other facilitating factors at work. For example, various EC countries (especially those that had not been major empire-builders during the heyday of European imperialism) began to feel that a sweeping multilateral relationship with the Third World could prove much more lucrative for them than functioning within a bilateral framework. Germany, which had minimal ties with such areas as Africa, was typical in this respect, viewing Lomé as a highly promising vehicle for gaining access to sub-Saharan markets and especially raw materials. Perhaps more important, however, was the specter of OPEC looming on the horizon. The Arab oil embargo associated with the 1973 Yom Kippur War was imposed shortly after the Lomé negotiations got under way, dramatically driving home to the Continent its dependence on Third World raw materials (see Table 3.3 for an example of EC reliance on LDCs for minerals) and thereby generating an environment of intense concern about the reliability of future supplies. In short, the embargo created both objective and subjective conditions within the EC whereby the Third World was increasingly recognized as crucial to the Community's economic security, which in turn meant that the concept of long-term agreements (even at the cost of some heretofore unpalatable concessions) became much more attractive to the Europeans. Accordingly, the first Lomé Convention was signed on February 28, 1975, and went into effect on April 1, 1976.

Table 3.3 EC Imports of Minerals from Africa, 1974–1976 Average

	Percentage of Total EC Imports
Asbestos	15.0
Antimony	14.0
Chromium ore	34.0
Cobalt ore	94.0
Cobalt ore unwrought	63.0
Ferromanganese	29.0
Ferrochrome	46.0
Gold	46.0
Manganese metal	80.0
Manganese ore	80.0
Phosphates	61.0
Platinum and alloys unwrought	40.0
Tin (concentrates and metal)	15.5
Vanadium pentoxide	42.0

Source: L.L.C. Smets, "European Minerals Policy: Investing in Stability?" (paper presented at the Conference on the European Community, the Third World and the United Nations, Ralph Bunche Institute, City University of New York, March 17–18, 1978), p. 17.

The four primary issue-areas addressed by Lomé I were commerce, financial and technical aid, industrial cooperation, and institutional structures and relationships. The two key trade provisions were duty-free access to the EC for practically all (i.e., 99 percent) ACP goods, and STABEX, which was essentially an indexing scheme designed to stabilize the earnings of twelve basic ACP products exported to the Community. In addition, separate protocols focusing on long-term quota or price agreements were negotiated covering bananas, rum, and sugar, the last being the most crucial to the West Indies. There was nothing particularly novel in the financial and technical assistance programs; they fell well within the general contours of established western foreign aid efforts, with most of the money involved being channeled through the European Development Fund and the European Investment Bank. Industrial collaboration was treated as a separate Lomé item, although conceptually there was little difference between it and the activities falling under the rubric of financial and technical assistance. The main ACP goals in the industrial realm included diversification of domestic production, technology transfer, and the development of greater marketing expertise in the export sector, with the Fund and the Bank once again playing central roles. Finally, as might be expected in an endeavor encompassing over fifty nations, four major geographical areas, and numerous functional fields, the organizational structure that emerged to oversee the Lomé regimes was quite complex. While admittedly simplifying the situation somewhat, Figure 3.5 schematically summarizes its main components.

Figure 3.5 Basic Outline of the Lomé Organizational Structure

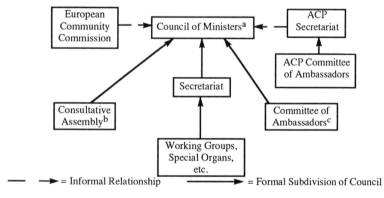

[a]Composed of members of the Council of the EEC, members of the EC Commission, and a member of the government of each ACP state.
[b]Consists of members of the European Parliament and representatives appointed by ACP states, with both sides having the same number of delegates.
[c]Consists of a representative of the EC Commission and representives from each EC/ACP country.

Although not formal elements of the Lomé structure, both the EC Commission and the ACP Secretariat are deeply involved in monitoring the implementation of the accords and especially in negotiating the terms of renewal every five years. They are, therefore, crucial players in the overall dynamics of the Lomé process.[42]

Lomé I certainly did not prove to be an unqualified success evaluated from a Third World perspective. Some important precedents had, of course, been set (e.g., the EC agreed in principle to respect sovereign equality in implementing and administering as well as negotiating the package), and material benefits were forthcoming in such areas as financial and technical cooperation. But counterbalancing the positive gains was the growing realization (and frustration) of the ACP that, says John Ravenhill,

> nothing in the relationship was *guaranteed*. The Convention was riddled with diverse escape clauses that permitted the Community to abrogate the agreement for reasons ranging from "the protection of health and life of humans, animals, and plants," to an insufficiency of funds (STABEX scheme). And there was nothing to prevent the Community from unilaterally redefining the "special relationship" by extending its benefits to third parties. . . . Although the Community was obliged under the terms of the Convention to inform the ACP and consult with them "where the Contracting Parties envisage taking any trade measures affecting the interest of one or more Contracting Parties," its compliance with this obligation seldom extended beyond a token gesture.[43]

Nevertheless, despite such apparently glaring defects, the Lomé scenario remained attractive enough to merit continuation when the first five-year phase was completed.

The most contentious issue in the Lomé II discussions, which formally began on July 24, 1978, revolved around the nature rather than the specifics of the process. The EC delegation perceived the talks essentially as an exercise in renewing the existing understandings. There might be, they conceded, a need for some revisions in projects already under way, but basically they wanted to continue within the general framework established by Lomé I. The ACP countries, on the other hand, insisted that almost the entire relationship had to be considered open for renegotiation in order to remedy what they felt were some fundamental flaws. Moreover, although they did not express it in these postdependency terms, it appeared that they were in a larger sense seeking to create a vehicle that would be effective not only in helping them to make and consolidate a transition to controlled dependence, but also in promoting an international environment conducive to their acquisition of structural power.

These widely divergent viewpoints resulted in protracted and often acrimonious consultations, with tensions becoming so strained that the talks seemed to have reached a total impasse by May 1979. Eventually, however, an understanding was reached, on October 31, 1979, that essentially reflected the EC position. The Europeans did, of course, make some concessions— certain trade provisions were liberalized in the ACP's favor, STABEX was improved and extended, and cooperative arrangements were instituted in such new areas as migrant workers, fishing, and shipping. But overall the Lomé II accords offered little to those Third World leaders interested in a fundamental reconfiguration of the international economic-political order; they simply did not incorporate the kind of radical innovations from which structural power can flow. In short, the bargaining process produced here what it does in the great majority of cases—a fairly modest agreement that falls far short of one party's expectations but nevertheless contains enough benefits for everyone involved that it is much preferable to no agreement at all.

The Lomé III experience (1985) was in many respects quite similar to its immediate predecessor. In particular, the main stress once again was on fine-tuning the edifice that had been constructed over the past ten years rather than plunging into the uncharted (and, in the EEC's opinion, dangerous) waters of new paradigms. Consequently the agenda continued to revolve around such concerns as refining STABEX, exploring various mechanisms to provide preferential entry to European markets for ACP products (especially commodities), and arguing over the levels of financial support necessary to effectively implement the various facets of the Lomé package.

There were, however, several new factors in the equation that complicated matters somewhat during this round, particularly for the Third World camp. For instance, the ACP ranks had swelled from the original forty-six members to sixty-six participants by 1985. While this expansion had its potential assets in the sense that it at least theoretically made the Lomé process more attractive to the Europeans because they were now afforded the opportunity to establish special long-term economic relationships with approximately half of the world's countries, it also represented a logistical liability, since many more national interests now had to be accommodated before the ACP could present a united front. Also, and perhaps most important, the negotiating climate of the mid-1980s was not as hospitable to the Third World as had been the case a decade earlier; the Europeans were no longer psychologically intimidated by OPEC or the fear of major raw materials shortages; conversely, the LDCs were not anxious for a major confrontation with the North because they were in the midst of a severe economic crisis characterized by escalating debts and declining productivity. The ACP states realized that, if Lomé were to play a significant role in helping them to escape the economic quagmire in which they were trapped, its performance would have to improve considerably in such areas as trade, where the data indicated that their relative position in the European market had in fact deteriorated (e.g., in 1975 the original forty-six ACP nations supplied 20 percent of the EC's imports as compared to only 14 percent for the sixty-six ACP members in 1985).[44] Under such conditions, pragmatism demanded that the LDCs concentrate on strengthening the Lomé III framework with the hope of improving their economic situation and future bargaining position. Thus, reform of the existing structure rather than the creation of a new one characterized the ACP approach to the Lomé III negotiations.

The CARICOM states were heavily involved in the Lomé process from the very beginning. Indeed, in many instances they played a vanguard role in trying to foster greater South-South unity in order to strengthen the Third World's bargaining position vis-à-vis the EC. Such assertiveness was especially evident in the initiatives involved in promoting and negotiating the first set of Lomé accords.

Once Britain's entry to the EC was formalized by the January 1972 Treaty of Accession, the West Indians moved swiftly to formulate their response. In mid-1972, for example, a high-powered Caribbean delegation toured Africa to solicit opinions and ideas regarding possible scenarios available to the Commonwealth now that they could no longer negotiate their special economic relations directly with London but rather had to deal with the EC as a whole. The West Indian position was officially announced at the seventh Heads of Commonwealth Caribbean Governments Conference, which took place in Trinidad in October 1972. The nine-point program that was adopted dealt mostly with West Indian concerns, although close cooperation with Africa was specifically mentioned.[45] It was, however, unclear at this point whether the Commonwealth Caribbean would as a region deal directly with the EC or would choose instead to operate as a partner within a larger Third World negotiating coalition, for there were strong lobbies behind each alternative. Ultimately the latter option carried the day at the eighth Heads of Government convocation in Guyana (April 1973), with one of its chief advocates—Shridath (Sonny) Ramphal of Guyana—being designated as the Caribbean's chief representative in the process.

Once they definitively committed themselves to a united front, the West Indians quickly became a driving force behind the establishment and activities of the ACP group. In particular, Ramphal and his team collaborated closely with their African counterparts, with protocol as well as political considerations rooted in the numerical majority the sub-Saharan states enjoyed within the organization often leading the West Indians to adopt a fairly low public profile. Thus, for example, Ramphal, despite the fact that the Caribbean contingent had done much of the substantive preparatory work, deferred to the selection of an African dignitary to serve as the ACP's official spokesman in the initial 1973 negotiations with the EC. Behind the scenes, however, the West Indians were invariably exerting immense

influence due to their technical expertise and sophisticated diplomatic skills.
Indeed, says Ellen Frey-Wouters,

> From the start of the [Lomé I] negotiations, the Caribbean group caught the
> attention of the other negotiators. The 18 months of talks showed the group
> to be tough and effective. . . . Jamaica and Guyana in particular played a
> leadership role.
>   The Caribbean countries also expressed their continuing solidarity
> with the aspirations of the Third World. In their view, the relationship with
> the EEC should contain no features that would debar or inhibit them from
> establishing and strengthening economic integration and cooperation
> agreements with other Third World countries. There was a strong belief,
> especially in Guyana and Jamaica, that only a new international economic
> order would give poor nations a substantially greater share of the world's
> wealth.[46]

Basically then, as Frey-Wouters's comments suggest, the West Indian
perspective went far beyond the use of a collective bargaining strategy to
achieve an ACP agreement with the EC. Rather, the whole Lomé process
was seen and approached within a much larger framework of South-South
relations and postdependency politics where the ultimate goal was structural
transformation involving radical redistribution of economic-political power
at the global level.

After the Lomé I accords were reached the CARICOM states shifted
their attention to the creation of the institutional vehicles they felt were
necessary to maximize the ACP's coordinative capacity and its ability to
effectively monitor the implementation of the Lomé provisions. Accordingly
a conference was convened in Guyana, where on June 6, 1975, the
Georgetown Agreement was adopted. What emerged from this document
was in effect a mirror image of the upper levels of the Lomé organizational
chart—specifically, an ACP Council of Ministers, an ACP Committee of
Ambassadors, and an ACP Secretariat were established. The Secretariat soon
emerged as the nerve center of this system, its prominence resting mainly on
two pillars: first, it was delegated primary responsibility under the
Georgetown Agreement for the day-to-day promotion and protection of the
group's interests; and second, member governments were usually willing to
defer to the advice of the solid core of extremely capable technocrats that it
attracted.

The Secretariat has traditionally been a key conduit through which
CARICOM influence is channeled into the ACP mainstream, the
transmission belt being the large number of West Indians who have served
on it and have often risen rapidly through its ranks. Consequently, in both the
Lomé II and III rounds, neither individual Caribbean governments nor
CARICOM as a distinct entity became heavily involved in the bargaining
process in a direct manner. Indeed, in Lomé II's case, the CARICOM

Council of Ministers took the somewhat unusual step of announcing beforehand that it had decided to limit the CARICOM Secretariat (normally the organization's main operational link to the ACP structure) to a minor role in the upcoming negotiations. This policy was indicative of the confidence that the West Indians had and continue to have in their ability to capitalize on their well-established personnel beachhead within the ACP bureaucracy to play a vanguard Lomé role.

The Lomé Conventions unfortunately have not lived up to the initially high expectations held by the Caribbean states and their LDC associates. Among their major complaints are that trade provisions have not been liberalized sufficiently to allow Third World products to be truly competitive in European markets, as evidenced by the drop in the ACP's share of EC imports; that Europe's commitment to financial and technical cooperation has been inadequate, with the real per capita aid figures actually declining (e.g., by approximately 5–7 percent from Lomé II to Lomé III); that there is no mechanism for arbitrating disputes that might arise under the accords; and finally, that the Europeans have failed to demonstrate in practice the concept of sovereign equality they have embraced in principle, unfortunately continuing to behave as patrons rather than partners.[47] Less jaded observers, on the other hand, while not disputing the fact that the Lomé accords often fell short of their announced goals, were more generous in their evaluations, stressing in their performance equations the dysfunctional international environment confronting the developing nations in general and the Lomé scenario in particular. In a nutshell, what was being suggested was that the Lomé Conventions were to a significant degree the victims of poor timing, since they were implemented during a period (i.e., the late 1970s and the 1980s) when the developmental posture of practically all Third World countries was eroding dramatically. Indeed in many instances the situation became truly desperate as LDCs experienced plummeting prices for their commodity exports, escalating costs for their petroleum and other imports, reduced markets abroad for their goods, high levels of inflation, and a burgeoning foreign debt crisis. Probably the most that one could expect the Lomé accords to accomplish under such difficult conditions would be to provide some disaster insurance against the economic whirlwinds that were rampaging through the Third World. While it obviously is impossible to say exactly what would have occurred had the Lomé arrangements not existed, it likewise is certain that the ACP Group would have been in much more dire straits without them. It was, of course, extremely distasteful within CARICOM circles to have to redefine Lomé in terms of preventing things from getting worse rather than guaranteeing that they would improve considerably, for no one likes to abandon (even temporarily) his visions of a better future. Given the circumstances, however, it was probably the only realistic alternative.

The fact that the ACP states had to curtail their aspirations was not, as pessimists might be tempted to conclude, the functional equivalent of a death knell for Lomé. To the contrary, despite frustrations and undeniable performance shortfalls, formalization of the EEC–ACP link through multilateral diplomacy had by the mid-1980s become an institutionalized feature of the international landscape. Admittedly the vicissitudes of the larger global system too often have had, at least from an LDC perspective, a negative impact on the concrete results of the discussions, and progress has been painfully slow on some issues. Yet these problems should not be allowed to overshadow the fact that the very survival of the Lomé process (which included a fourth-round agreement in 1990) stands as graphic evidence of a major Third World–Caribbean accomplishment—the acquisition and exercise of collective bargaining power within the context of periodic negotiations over the exact terms of at least some important aspects of the North-South relationship. In short, Lomé demonstrates that the South-South option can be a viable vehicle for making strides toward the controlled dependence state of the postdependency continuum.

Notes

1. The material in this section draws heavily from Elizabeth Wallace, *The British Caribbean: From the Decline of Colonialism to the End of Federation* (Toronto, Ont.: University of Toronto Press, 1977), chs. 5–8. See also Sir John Modecai, *Federation of the West Indies* (Evanston, IL: Northwestern University Press, 1968).

2. The current members of CARICOM achieved independence in this order: Jamaica and Trinidad and Tobago in 1962; Barbados and Guyana in 1966; the Bahamas in 1973; Grenada in 1974; Dominica in 1978; St. Lucia and St. Vincent and the Grenadines in 1979; Antigua and Barbuda and Belize in 1981; and St. Kitts–Nevis in 1983. Montserrat is still a UK dependency.

3. See, e.g., William G. Demas, *The Political Economy of the English-Speaking Caribbean: A Summary View* (Port of Spain, Trinidad: Caribbean Ecumenical Consultation, Study Paper no. 4, 1971); and Vernon Choudra Mulchansingh, *CARIFTA: New Horizons in the West Indies* (Mona, Jamaica: University of the West Indies, Department of Geography, Occasional Publications no. 3, 1968).

4. A good summary of these two schools of thought is in W. Andrew Axline, *Caribbean Integration: The Politics of Regionalism* (New York: Nichols, 1979), pp. 84–87.

5. After protracted negotiations complicated by the lack of a strong domestic consensus on the issue, the United Kingdom finally joined the EC in 1973. The concerns expressed by the West Indies as well as other Third World members of the British Commonwealth about their "most favored nation" trade status were addressed in the Lomé accords, discussed later in this chapter.

6. Although they joined CARIFTA, the WISA states continued to pursue their activities within the ECCM. In essence, then, CARIFTA constituted a twelve-nation free trade area within which seven of the associates operated a subregional common

market. For details regarding the rather complex developmental history of, and relationships between, those various bodies, see Axline, *Caribbean Integration,* pp. 83–89 and 99–101.

7. Ibid., p. 89.

8. Economic Commission for Latin America, Office for the Caribbean, *The Caribbean Integration Programme: 1968–1972* (Port of Spain, 1973 draft), p. 19.

9. Anthony Bryan, "The CARICOM and Latin American Integration Experiences: Observations on Theoretical Origins and Comparative Performance," in *Ten Years of CARICOM* (Washington, DC: Inter-American Development Bank, 1984), p. 75.

10. For details, see CARICOM Secretariat, *From CARIFTA to Caribbean Community* (Georgetown, Guyana: CARICOM, 1972), pp. 65–78; and CARICOM Secretariat, *The Caribbean Community—A Guide* (Georgetown, Guyana: CARICOM, 1973), pp. 7–15.

11. Quoted in Axline, *Caribbean Integration,* p. 117.

12. The Bahamas was not one of the original members of CARICOM. Instead, it first assumed a stance that might be best described as observer status and then gradually became more actively involved in the organization. Finally, it became a formal participant in July 1983.

13. Two of the pioneering works in functionalist theory are Ernst Haas, *Beyond the Nation-State* (Stanford, CA: Stanford University Press, 1964); and David Mitrany, *A Working Peace System* (Chicago: Quadrangle Books, 1966).

14. Bryan, "CARICOM and Latin American Integration," p. 87.

15. Axline, *Caribbean Integration,* p. 78.

16. Odette Jankowitsch and Karl P. Sauvant, "The Initiating Role of the Non-Aligned Countries," in Karl P. Sauvant, ed., *Changing Priorities on the International Agenda: The New International Economic Order* (New York: Pergamon Press, 1981), pp. 66–67.

17. United Nations General Assembly resolutions 3201 (S-VI) and 3202 (S-VI), adopted May 1, 1974.

18. The nineteen fields of activity wherein the coordinating countries try to stimulate South-South cooperation are international cooperation for development; trade, transport, and industry; financial and monetary cooperation; scientific and technological development; technical cooperation and consultancy services; food and agriculture; fisheries; telecommunications; insurance; health; employment and human resources development; tourism; transnational corporations; sports; raw materials; research and information systems; ad hoc group for the Solidarity Fund for Economic and Social Development; role of women in development; and peaceful uses of nuclear energy.

19. Lloyd Searwar, "Non-Alignment as a Viable Alternative for Regional Cooperation" (paper presented at a March 1982 seminar, "Geo-Political Change in the Caribbean in the 1980s," Georgetown, Guyana), p. 7.

20. In order to make it easier for LDCs to selectively delink from metropolitan centers as part of the NIEO process, Manley unveiled a plan at the Algiers Summit calling for the establishment of a Third World fund to be underwritten by the more prosperous nonaligned countries (especially those in OPEC whose oil resources could be transformed into large reserves of petrodollars). Such a facility would have the potential, he argued, to reduce significantly the dependency of many developing nations on the industrialized West in general and western-dominated financial institutions in particular.

21. Winston E. Langley, "From Manley to Seaga: Changes in Jamaican Foreign Policy," *Transition* 8 (1983): 5.

22. The total Latin American–Caribbean contingent in the NAM as of 1983 (entry dates are in parentheses) was Argentina (1973), Bahamas (1983), Barbados (1983), Belize (1983), Bolivia (1979), Chile (1973), Colombia (1983), Cuba (1961), Ecuador (1983), Grenada (1979), Guyana (1970), Jamaica (1970), Nicaragua (1979), Panama (1976), Peru (1973), St. Lucia (1983), Suriname (1979), and Trinidad and Tobago (1970). Chile boycotted the Movement after being criticized at the 1976 Colombo Summit. Thus, even though technically a member of the NAM, it was not invited to attend any of the organization's functions.

In addition to the regular members, the Latin American–Caribbean countries affiliated with the NAM as permanent observers at this time were Antigua, Brazil, Costa Rica, El Salvador, Mexico, Uruguay, and Venezuela.

See *NACLA Report on the Americas* 19, no. 3 (May–June 1985): 16.

23. For details concerning the rivalry between radical and moderate blocs, see Roger D. Hansen, *Beyond the North/South Stalemate* (New York: McGraw-Hill, 1979), pp. 44–51; and H. Michael Erisman, "Cuba and the Third World: The Nonaligned Nations Movement," in Barry B. Levine, ed., *The New Cuban Presence in the Caribbean* (Boulder, CO: Westview Press, 1983), pp. 149–170.

24. For general background on the NWIO issue, see Anthony Smith, *The Geopolitics of Information: How Western Culture Dominates the World* (New York: Oxford University Press, 1980); and Thomas L. McPhail, *Electronic Colonialism: The Future of International Broadcasting and Communication* (Beverly Hills, CA: Space Publications, 1981). Details regarding Guyana's participation in the Djakarta meeting are summarized in "Information Imbalance: A Pattern of Inequity," *Guyana Chronicle* (January 27, 1984) and "Cooperation not Confrontation," *Guyana Chronicle* (January 28, 1984).

25. Leelananda de Silva, "The Non-Aligned Movement: Its Economic Organization and NIEO Perspectives," in Breda Pavlic, Raúl R. Uranga, Boris Cizelj, and Marjan Svetlicic, eds., *The Challenges of South-South Cooperation* (Boulder, CO: Westview Press, 1983), p. 76.

26. As of 1981, the UNCTAD division's fourteen permanent working groups were the Group of 33 on the Integrated Programme for Common Fund, Group of 15 on Institutional Questions, Group of 30 on Economic Co-operation among Developing Countries, Group of 15 on Monetary and Financial Issues, Co-ordinating Committee on Multilateral Trade Negotiations, Group of 15 on Transfer of Technology, Group of 15 on International Development Strategy, Group of 15 on Manufacturing, Task Force of the Committee on Commodities, Group of 15 on the Least Developed Countries, Group of 21 on the Preparatory Commission on the Common Fund for Commodities, Group of 15 on Restrictive Business Practices, Group of 15 on Generalized System of Preferences, and Group of 15 on Shipping.

27. The nineteen Third World participants were Algeria, Argentina, Brazil, Cameroon, Egypt, India, Indonesia, Iran, Iraq, Jamaica, Mexico, Nigeria, Pakistan, Peru, Saudi Arabia, Venezuela, Yugoslavia, Zaire, and Zambia. The delegates representing the North were the EC (one seat for the organization as a whole), Australia, Canada, Japan, Spain, Sweden, Switzerland, and the United States.

28. The cochairmen were, for energy, Saudi Arabia and the United States; for raw materials, Japan and Peru; for development, Algeria and the EC; and for financial affairs, Iran and the EC. The CIEC as a whole also had cochairmen, which were Venezuela and Canada.

29. Robert A. Mortimer, *The Third World Coalition in International Politics* (Boulder, CO: Westview Press, 1984), p. 102. The summary material regarding the Paris Conference that is presented here comes from Mortimer, ch. 6, pp. 95–109.

30. The fourth precondition was that Cuba not be invited to the conference, a

demand many Third World governments felt was unreasonable (if not downright insulting), since Castro was at that time serving as the NAM's leader and therefore would normally have been expected to participate in that capacity. Havana decided not to push the issue to a confrontation, and hence Reagan was able to exclude the Fidelistas, whom he considered a potentially disruptive influence because he felt they were too radical and too anti-American.

31. Denis Benn, "The Commonwealth Caribbean and the New International Economic Order," in Anthony Payne and Paul Sutton, eds., *Dependency Under Challenge: The Political Economy of the Commonwealth Caribbean* (Manchester, Eng.: Manchester University Press, 1984), pp. 267–268.

32. In addition to Guyana, the other thirteen Third World States attending the Cancún summit were Algeria, Bangladesh, Brazil, China, India, Ivory Coast, Mexico, Nigeria, Philippines, Saudi Arabia, Tanzania, Venezuela, and Yugoslavia.

33. For an overview of the foreign policies of Caribbean Basin countries, see Anthony T. Bryan, "Las políticas exteriores de los estados de la mancomunidad del Caribe," in Juan Carlos Puig, ed., *América Latina: políticas exteriores comparados* (Buenos Aires: Grupo Editor Latinoamericano, 1984), pp. 236–265. More detailed analyses of Venezuelan and Mexican foreign policies can be found in John Martz, "Ideology and Oil: Venezuela in the Circum-Caribbean," and Edward J. Williams, "Mexico's Central American Policy: Revolutionary and Prudential Dimensions," both in H. Michael Erisman, ed., *Colossus Challenged: The Struggle for Caribbean Influence* (Boulder, CO: Westview Press, 1982), pp. 121–148 and 149–169 respectively.

34. Anthony T. Bryan, "CARICOM and Latin America," *NACLA Report on the Americas* 18, no. 6 (November–December 1984): 42–43.

35. The territorial disputes are discussed in Jacqueline Braveboy-Wagner, *The Venezuela-Guyana Border Dispute: Britain's Colonial Legacy in Latin America* (Boulder, CO: Westview Press, 1984); and Latin American Bureau, *The Belize Issue* (London: Latin American Bureau, 1978). The continuing animosity swirling around these disputes surfaced once again in 1983 when Guyana blocked Venezuela's bid to upgrade its status in the NAM from observer to full member. Subsequently, however, tensions between the two countries subsided, and consequently Caracas' NAM application was accepted in September 1989.

36. Luis Maira, "Caribbean State Systems and Middle Status Powers: The Cases of Mexico, Venezuela, and Cuba," in Paget Henry and Carl Stone, eds., *The Newer Caribbean: Decolonization, Democracy, and Development* (Philadelphia: Institute for the Study of Human Issues, 1983), p. 200.

37. For a macroanalysis of CARICOM voting patterns in the United Nations, see Jacqueline Braveboy-Wagner, *The Caribbean in World Affairs: The Foreign Policies of the English-Speaking States* (Boulder, CO: Westview Press, 1989), pp. 132–139.

38. Anthony T. Bryan, "The Commonwealth Caribbean/Latin American Relationship: New Wine in Old Bottles?" *Caribbean Affairs* 1, no. 1 (1988): 42.

39. The McComie case is discussed in "McComie Not in OAS Race," *Barbados Advocate* (March 12, 1984) and "Mutual Healing Effort Needed for OAS Rift," *Trinidad Guardian* (April 10, 1984), while information regarding the Barrow incident (as well as the quotation) comes from Tony Best, "Loss," *Caribbean Contact* (October 1988), pp. 1, 7.

40. An excellent overview of evolving Caribbean–Latin American cooperation, which concludes on a generally upbeat note, can be found in Andrés Serbín, "Race and Politics: Relations Between the English-Speaking Caribbean and Latin America," *Caribbean Affairs* 2, no. 4 (October–December 1989): 146–171.

41. Details regarding the negotiation and the substance of the Yaounde accords

can be found in John Ravenhill, *Collective Clientelism: The Lomé Conventions and North-South Relations* (New York: Columbia University Press, 1985), pp. 47–97.

42. These matters are discussed in much more detail in Ellen Frey-Wouters, *The European Community and the Third World: The Lomé Convention and Its Impact* (New York: Praeger Special Studies, 1980), pp. 36–79.

43. Ravenhill, *Collective Clientelism*, p. 310 (emphasis added).

44. These figures come from IRELA Conference Report no. 2/87, "The Caribbean Basin: Struggle for Independence, Democracy and Development, and the Role of Outside Powers" (Madrid: Institute for European–Latin American Relations [IRELA], 1987), p. 25.

45. The nine-point program is summarized in Paul Sutton, "From Neo-Colonialism to Neo-Colonialism: Britain and the EEC in the Commonwealth Caribbean," in Payne and Sutton, *Dependency Under Challenge*, p. 206, as follows:

1. Caribbean Free Trade Area (CARIFTA) countries should seek a group relationship with the EEC.
2. A *sui generis* relationship was required.
3. The focus of attention should be the content of the relationship rather than exercise of a particular option.
4. The relationship should provide for aid, at least for the LDCs.
5. CARIFTA should seek a secure and continuing market on the basis of an agreed Commonwealth quota for the supply of sugar to the enlarged EEC on fair terms in respect of quantities of sugar covered by the Commonwealth Sugar Agreement.
6. Commonwealth Caribbean governments must engage in intense diplomatic activity in Europe in order to convey the special problems of CARIFTA countries.
7. Invitations should be sent to representatives of the European Commission to visit CARIFTA countries early in 1973.
8. Closest cooperation should be developed with the African Associates (i.e. countries already associated under Yaounde II) and other Commonwealth associables.
9. The position of the dependent territories should be clarified.

46. Frey-Wouters, *European Community and the Third World*, p. 32.

47. These issues are discussed more fully in IRELA, "Caribbean Basin," pp. 23–30.

4

From Theory to Practice:
A Viability Analysis of CARICOM
South-South Postdependency Politics

We have concentrated thus far on two different dimensions of the postdependency equation: a broad conceptual overview of the topic and the historical evolution of South-South relations on CARICOM's part. In essence, then, what has been addressed is the conventional dichotomy of theory on the one hand and praxis on the other. The problem, of course, is that the latter does not necessarily flow smoothly from the former. Instead, there are inevitably intervening variables that can function either to facilitate or to hinder the transformation of ideas into reality. It is this interface between postdependency theory and productive South-South foreign policy behavior that now needs to be explored. Thus what follows is a viability analysis that seeks to examine some of the key factors that can operate to enhance or diminish the likelihood that CARICOM states will be willing and able to engage in South-South politics oriented toward acquiring the bargaining power required to make the postdependency transition to a system state of controlled dependence wherein they enjoy effective rather than merely formal sovereignty.

The essential ingredients of such an undertaking can, for simplicity's sake, be divided into two broad categories: (1) relatively short-term factors that are for the most part idiosyncratic to the West Indian situation; and (2) more general, long-term considerations whose impact may sometimes be limited to the Caribbean and in other cases may be relevant to the efforts of practically any developing nation to exercise the South-South post-dependency option. Most of our concern here is directed at the second set of variables, with the first set being incorporated into the concluding chapter's discussion of the contemporary dynamics of the CARICOM region's South-South relations and its postdependency prospects in the foreseeable future.

A further refinement of this scenario is mandated by the fact that specialists in international relations have long been sensitive to the need to discriminate between various levels of analysis,[1] the basic rationale being that the key actors and variables as well as the patterns of interaction between them will change as the focus of one's attention shifts. For example, the primary influences on the South-South affairs of CARICOM countries within a global forum such as the Nonaligned Movement are unlikely to be identical to those in the more limited arena of West Indian–Latin American relations. Recognizing the wisdom of making such distinctions, we use the following three-tiered framework for our viability inquiry.

1. The *macrosystemic level* refers to those factors influencing South-South postdependency politics that are related to the characteristics or dynamics of the international system as a whole, or to interactions between important components thereof. This is, in terms of political science systems theory, generally considered the most ambitious perspective that can be adopted, since its potential ramifications are truly global in scope and it normally demands attention to a large number of both independent and intervening variables no matter what the particular phenomenon under scrutiny.

2. The *LDC subsystemic level* refers to those factors influencing South-South postdependency politics that are related to the characteristics or dynamics of the developing world as a whole, or to interactions between important components thereof. In short, what is being surveyed here—either collectively or individually—are the major regional subsystems of the overall international system, with special emphasis being accorded to Latin America.

3. The *West Indian level* refers to those factors influencing South-South postdependency politics that originate or operate basically within the geopolitical confines of the Anglophone Caribbean.

Prudence cautions against attempting to scrutinize every conceivable variable that might appear at each analytical level; thus only those deemed the most important are reviewed here.

Facilitating Factors

Certainly the most dramatic development at the macrosystemic level during the waning years of the twentieth century is the major reconfiguration of global power that transpired during the 1980s and the early 1990s, the key element being the transition from the rather tight concentration that emerged after World War II to a much more flexible paradigm. This phenomenon has produced two key outcomes that bear significantly on the issue of South-South postdependency affairs: (1) the demise of strategic/military bipolarity, with special emphasis regarding its impact on the foreign policy perceptions and behavior of the two superpowers; and (2) the emergence of economic multipolarity.[2]

Tight strategic/military bipolarity is not, of course, conducive to initiatives by third parties. Instead, the paramount characteristic of such an environment is the smothering presence of the two dominant actors, who are locked in a power struggle to control as much of the international system as they possibly can. The specific mechanisms of control can range from the crudest forms of classical colonialism, whereby one country simply uses brute force to impose its rule on other territories and peoples, to the most subtle, yet still highly effective manifestations of dependency. In any case the role that this scenario assigns to most nations, especially those with size and/or resource problems that translate into high levels of external vulnerability, is hardly an enviable one. They tend to be perceived—both theoretically and certainly in the eyes of the superpowers—essentially as objects of control. Thus, any LDC's attempt to acquire and exercise bargaining power would not be likely to receive a very sympathetic reception. Indeed the historical record is filled with instances in which great powers have flexed their military or economic muscle to get rid of, rather than negotiate with (or even simply tolerate), governments that display an affinity for effective rather than merely formal sovereignty. Essentially, then, the political logic and psychological dynamics of tight military/strategic bipolarity lead inexorably to an international environment wherein significant political space is normally a luxury available only to the system's main actors.

During the heyday of the U.S.–Soviet Cold War, for example, it was extremely difficult for those nations located in an area considered by one of the superpowers to fall within its sphere of vital security interests to pursue their own independent agendas. Instead they were subjected to unremitting pressure for conformity to the dictates of Washington or Moscow. The West Indies were unfortunately among those who ran afoul of this harsh reality. Ever since the promulgation of the Monroe Doctrine in 1823, the United States has considered the Western Hemisphere in general and especially the Caribbean Basin to be its special bailiwick wherein it could enforce its law, its concept of acceptable socioeconomic-political order, and its code of international conduct. Consequently the CARICOM countries could not, as was the case with some Afro-Asian nations that also achieved independence during this period, capitalize on the Cold War by playing the superpowers off against one another.[3] Rather, West Indians found themselves in the extremely frustrating position of seeing the euphoria generated by the demise of British colonialism quickly dissipated by the increasingly long shadow cast over the region by the Colossus of the North.

The latter years of the twentieth century have, however, witnessed the unraveling of tight strategic/military bipolarity as both the White House and the Kremlin displayed a decreasing ability to dominate the world stage with their military power, the most dramatic manifestations of this phenomenon being the defeats inflicted on the United States in Vietnam and the USSR in Afghanistan. But perhaps equally important to this diminished objective capacity on the superpowers' part to dominate others through brute force was their waning subjective interest in doing so. The key to this process was a transformation of threat perceptions. In other words, a variety of factors led both superpowers to reassess the danger the other posed to its security and ultimately to conclude that its vital interests were no longer imperiled. This shift in the psychology of the superpower relationship from an emphasis on confrontationalism to accommodation (or détente), combined with the relative decline of U.S.–Soviet military influence, ushered in the demise of tight strategic/military bipolarity at the macrosystemic level of analysis.

The amelioration of East-West tensions that has accompanied the realignment of the international system's power configuration could enhance the prospects for the West Indies to move out from under the Yankee shadow, the basic premise being that the incentive for Washington to impose its will on others is inversely related to its view of the Kremlin as a security threat. U.S.–Soviet rapprochement has, in other words, opened up the world arena to other actors by reducing the perceived need as well as by removing a major rationale for the superpowers to maintain hegemonic control over their respective blocs. Such conditions should, for the most part, be quite positive for small countries such as those in the Caribbean, interjecting a significant element of "permissibility" into their foreign policies. Admittedly there may in certain instances be a downside, one example being the reduced probability within such a global environment that some nations will be able to implement the superclient option. In general, however, the passing of tight military/strategic bipolarity and its collateral U.S.–Soviet Cold War is likely to translate into opportunities for the CARICOM states to acquire markedly increased political space within which to pursue a South-South postdependency strategy.

The passing of strategic/military bipolarity could, of course, conceivably result in little more than a shift to economic tools of control as Washington's preferred mechanism for dominating the Caribbean. Certainly the West Indies' traditionally high degree of vulnerability to almost all forms of exogenous penetration not only seems to invite such a move, but also practically to guarantee its success. Yet what appears at first glance to be a plausible scenario becomes more complicated and problematical when the economic multipolarity that has emerged at the macrosystemic level is factored into the equation.

Understandably, perhaps, the melodrama surrounding the decline of strategic bipolarity has tended to divert attention from the fact that an even more fundamental change in the nature of the contemporary global arena has occurred: specifically, economic strength has surfaced to at least equal and perhaps even to displace armed force as the preeminent element of status and authority in the modern world. Japan is in the vanguard of this trend; it has become recognized as one of the key players in the game of nations even though its army, navy, and air force are small by normal great power standards and it spends relatively little on defense, preferring instead to channel its resources into high-technology industrial development. Others have followed similar paths, according greater priority to economic than to military concerns and emerging in the process as new centers of international influence. Consequently multipolar economic power rather than bipolar military might has in many respects come to be the defining hallmark of the international system in the late twentieth century.

Beyond the fairly obvious fact that this situation presents an opportunity for the CARICOM nations to capitalize on what bargaining power the South-South option might furnish to diversify their North-South linkages by establishing firm ties that extend beyond their traditional industrialized trading partners (e.g., Great Britain and the United States), there likewise could be a strong push factor at work in the sense that LDCs may find themselves increasingly constrained to embrace the principle of collective action in order to be able to deal effectively with the powerful economic conglomerates that multipolarity has tended to spawn. Desmond Hoyte, the president of Guyana, highlighted the urgency involved when he warned in 1989 that

> a pervasive feature of international relations today is the politics of economic regionalism, which derives from the emergence of powerful economic blocs in the world. . . . I think the inference to be drawn from all these developments is quite clear; we must avoid the temptation of believing that we can act individually even to protect our individual national interests. Huge economic groupings are going to dominate the world economy and there will be no place for countries that try to go it alone. Certainly the member states of CARICOM cannot face the powerful groupings individually. We have to combine our forces to obtain maximum leverage in any negotiations with them.[4]

Particularly worrisome to the West Indies is the planned establishment of a free trade area (commonly referred to as a common market) encompassing the United States, Canada, and Mexico, with a merger of the U.S. and Canadian legs of the triad arousing the greatest trepidation. This concern is rooted in the fact that historically the separate existence of these two countries as major trading partners interjected a crucial element of diversity in CARICOM's export-import picture, assuring that the possibility—if not necessarily the reality—of "shopping around" for the best deal always existed. Not only, therefore, did the prospect of greater Caribbean decisionmaking flexibility arise, but perhaps most important was the concomitant sense of psychological security that tends to flow from the belief that options are available over which one can truly exercise some control.

A North American common market would put the CARICOM countries in a weakened position because it would force them to negotiate with a single megabloc rather than individual parties. An obvious response, of course, would be to fight consolidation with consolidation by promoting the adoption of a collective bargaining strategy by all LDCs (in the Western Hemisphere or elsewhere) confronted with the specter of having to adapt to the formation of a North American free trade area. This principle should likewise be applicable in comparable cases, which in effect means that economic integration of industrialized nations must be recognized as a characteristic of the contemporary international system that can serve as a major motivating factor behind the South-South postdependency politics of the West Indies and other developing states.

Turning to the LDC subsystemic level of analysis, it is within the context of western hemispheric affairs that the most important variables promoting or facilitating CARICOM South-South postdependency politics can be found. As has been the case in the Anglophone Caribbean, many Latin American states are highly sensitive to the potential dangers inherent in the tendency toward the proliferation of amalgamated power centers that macrosystemic multilateralism fosters. The need to mount a counteroffensive has reinvigorated sympathy for the concept of Latin American unity. However, in contrast to previous manifestations of such sentiment, there has been an increasing inclination on the Hispanics' part to include the CARICOM countries. Indeed, says Andrés Serbín, who is perhaps the foremost authority on this subject,

> the Caribbean has begun to emerge [in Latin American eyes] as an attractive trade and financial option, not only in terms of local markets, but also as a means for access to the North American and European markets through the CBI [the U.S. Caribbean Basin Initiative program] and the Lomé Agreement. There is also a perception of the need for reinforcing a concerted regional policy in regard to negotiations with the economic mega-blocs of the North.[5]

The "Big Three" of the Basin—Venezuela, Mexico, and Colombia—have been considered by most observers the natural candidates to serve as the main bridges between the mainland and the non-Hispanic Caribbean, with Caracas generally displaying the most enthusiasm for the idea.

The pan-Caribbean perspectives of Mexico and Venezuela assumed significant policy implications in the 1970s when, buoyed both materially and psychologically by the massive influx of petrodollars generated by

OPEC's activities, the two countries developed aspirations to play much more assertive roles in the region. Numerous initiatives were launched to enhance their influence, one good example being the 1980 San José accords whereby Mexico and Venezuela pledged to provide oil at preferential prices to various Central American and Caribbean states (i.e., Barbados, Jamaica, and Haiti). Specifically, notes John Martz,

> Venezuela and Mexico collectively promised up to 160,000 barrels per day; credits would be granted equal to 30 percent of the cost of oil purchases for a five-year period at 4 percent interest annually. If a recipient could demonstrate the use of the loan for internal energy development, the repayment period would be stretched over twenty years with interest rates halved to 2 percent. . . . The accord also promised measurable assistance to the recipients who, even in the event of sharp price increases, would be favored by such easy loans, by the security of supply, and by modest shipping costs.[6]

Normally the impact of such overtures would not have been too significant, but during the 1970s and early 1980s the United States and Western European nations were not as economically formidable as before. Instead, most of these countries were experiencing serious problems as inflation and unemployment soared while trade balances turned heavily negative under OPEC's escalation of oil prices and stiff competition from industrialized Asia in the steel, automotive, textile, and consumer electronics markets. Indeed Washington was even forced to abandon certain aspects of its cherished Bretton Woods system, such as fixed rates of international currency exchange. It was increasingly difficult under such conditions for the United States to control its dependent periphery, and hence countries such as those in the CARICOM region found that they now had the leeway to explore new opportunities for diversified economic relations (e.g., the Mexico-Venezuela petroleum deal) that were becoming available.

The West Indian response to such South-South overtures from the Hispanics was for the most part favorable. As might be expected, CARICOM members traditionally in the postdependency vanguard (i.e., Guyana, Jamaica, and Trinidad and Tobago) seized quickly upon the opportunities presented to diversity their economic ties and hoped to lay a firm foundation for enhancing their bargaining power. But, interestingly enough, so also did Caribbean countries not normally credited with having any significant hemispheric vision. Thus, by the mid-1980s the Bahamas had taken steps to expand trade with Brazil, Mexico, and Panama while in Antigua's case 21 percent of its total 1984 exports went to Latin America. Moreover, concludes Jacqueline Braveboy-Wagner, based on her analysis of 1988 International Monetary Fund data, these trends continued into the latter part of the decade.[7] The early 1990s saw Mexico, plagued by massive debts and increasingly prone to seek salvation in closer ties with Washington, somewhat downgrading the Caribbean's priority on its international agenda. The Venezuelans, on the other hand, have continued to promote collaboration vigorously.[8] They have, for example, acquired observer status in CARICOM and have launched various developmental programs with its members, two illustrations being a 1990 energy agreement with Guyana that extends preferential treatment to Georgetown in purchasing electricity as well as petroleum[9] and a July 1990 announcement of plans to build an oil refinery in Grenada.[10]

Certainly a key development that could bode well for the future of CARICOM–Latin American cooperation in the pursuit of controlled dependence is the progress that has been made in defusing some of the tensions that various territorial disputes have generated. Admittedly nothing definitive has transpired in the two most serious controversies—Guatemala versus Belize and Venezuela against Guyana—but signs indicating that a more optimistic outlook is warranted do exist. Belize and Guatemala have, for instance, now consented to the creation of a mixed commission to help narrow the negotiating gap between them and to expedite further dialog. Caracas and Georgetown have traveled even farther down the road toward full reconciliation, having agreed to turn over responsibility for choosing the specific mechanisms to be used in settling their differences to the United Nations' secretary-general. Finally, setting a standard for accommodation that many hope others will emulate, Venezuela and Trinidad and Tobago resolved a complex, volatile quarrel centering on the Gulf of Paria[11] by signing, in 1990, marine boundary delimitation accords establishing exclusive economic zones for each country as well as clearly defining their respective fishing rights. Such pragmatism and compromises can, of course, be conducive to the expansion of South-South postdependency politics in the Western Hemisphere by helping to engender an atmosphere devoid of the confrontational psychology that too often in the past has characterized and poisoned the dynamics of CARICOM–Latin American relations.

Another crucial variable operating at the hemispheric subsystemic level that could cause the West Indies to look more seriously toward Latin America to find partners in postdependency politics is the rather meager benefits produced by the CBI. The CBI, as was the case with the more ambitious Alliance for Progress of the 1960s, was conceived by the Reagan administration as a means to counter what was seen to be a growing leftist threat to the prevailing pro-western ideological order and U.S. influence in the Caribbean Basin.[12] The first blow to Washington's complacent assumption that the area constituted a docile backyard came in March 1979 when a band of young radicals led by Maurice Bishop staged the West Indies' first successful armed coup, in Grenada. Four months later (July 1979), the Sandinistas marched triumphantly in Managua, thus breaking the

Somoza dynasty's long stranglehold on Nicaragua. The October 1980 Jamaican election in which conservative Edward Seaga defeated incumbent socialist Michael Manley was unusually bloody, with approximately 745 people dying in campaign-related violence (a comparable body count in the United States would be about 78,200). Other Anglophone countries displaying some proclivity for radical violence during this period were Dominica, St. Lucia, and St. Vincent. Finally, both El Salvador and Guatemala were plunging deeper into chaos as leftist-led insurgents escalated their guerrilla wars against the two countries' pro–United States governments. The CBI was the Reaganites' attempt to bring U.S. economic power to bear in order to help pacify the region.

Three basic elements were incorporated into the CBI, which became fully functional in 1983 after having been formally proposed in February 1982. First, the flow of U.S. government developmental aid was increased. The initial package called for a $350 million emergency grant for 1982 followed by $750 million over the next three years (with administration officials clearly implying that more would be forthcoming if needed). Second, most Caribbean exports entering the U.S. market were guaranteed duty-free status for twelve years. And finally, in what probably was the provision most dear to the White House, arrangements designed to promote private investment in the Basin were made that included various tax and financial incentives for U.S. companies and even formal bilateral treaties to protect their holdings (especially against nationalization and other forms of "unacceptable" governmental intervention in their affairs).

The CBI's promise to provide a special and highly beneficial relationship with the United States was, despite the pessimism voiced in some quarters, greeted enthusiastically in the English-speaking Caribbean. This situation aroused some concern among advocates of greater CARICOM–Latin American cooperation, for they recognized that the CBI had immense potential to rivet the attention and developmental expectations of any nation surveying the hemispheric landscape on the United States rather than the Hispanic countries. Indeed, to the extent that the CBI was perceived as a panacea for the West Indies' economic problems, much (if not all) of the rationale and incentive for South-South solidarity with Latin America would be in serious jeopardy of becoming irrelevant. Such fears proved, however, to be somewhat premature as it became increasingly evident that the program was not living up to its rhetoric.

While there have been some bright spots, the most dramatic successes involving the stimulation of nontraditional Caribbean exports into the U.S. market, the broad balance sheet has come under withering fire.[13] Typical of the critics is David Lewis, who, referring to the CBI's impact on all its participating countries (not just the West Indies), observes that "over the 1985–1989 period the U.S. increased its exports to the Caribbean Basin by

6.4 percent while Caribbean Basin exports to the U.S. fell by 5.2 percent over the same period. As such, the region has developed a trade deficit with the U.S. in the amount of $1.5 billion and become the only region with whom the U.S. has a trade surplus."[14]

The picture that emerges when we focus solely on the CARICOM countries is not quite as bleak, but still the general pattern during the late 1980s was one of decline in several key areas where CBI advocates had projected steady growth in benefits. Specifically, says Anthony González, the healthy trade surplus that the West Indies once enjoyed with the United States was severely eroded (Table 4.1) and U.S. aid to the region dropped significantly (Table 4.2), with the member countries of the OECS, who had counted on strong support to expand their weak developmental infrastructures, among the hardest-hit.[15]

Table 4.1 U.S. Trade Balance with CARICOM CBI–Designated Countries (in Millions of U.S. Dollars)

	1984	1985	1986	1987
Imports	2,193	1,930	1,397	1,453
Exports	1,560	1,307	1,385	1,363
Deficit/Surplus	633	613	12	90

Source: U.S. Department of Commerce, Official Statistics.

Table 4.2 U.S. Aid Flows to CARICOM States (in Millions of U.S. Dollars)

	1984	1985	1986	1987	1988[a]
Eastern Caribbean	106	54	49	49	46
Jamaica	108	155	119	78	95
Total	214	209	168	127	141

Source: U.S. Department of State Bulletin.
[a]Proposed by U.S. administration.

Although a revised and expanded version of the program—popularly termed CBI II—was instituted in 1990, there is considerable skepticism that it will be able to produce any major reversals in the rather lackluster overall performance recorded by its predecessor.

It therefore seems justified to say that the CBI has been demythologized; no longer can one blithely assume (or perhaps even just hope) that Washington and a posse of U.S. entrepreneurs stand ready to ride to the Caribbean's rescue. Inherent within this situation may lie the seeds of increased West Indian–Latin American cooperation, for a clear conclusion that could be drawn therefrom is that CARICOM's Hispanic neighbors represent excellent potential suppliers of the help it needs with regard to finding new trade and aid opportunities and negotiating the future terms of its economic relations with the United States. Hence, in a paradoxical twist of fate, what was originally envisioned by Washington as a mechanism to enhance its influence over the West Indies may actually be seen as encouraging hemispheric postdependency politics.

When we probe the West Indian level of analysis for factors conducive to CARICOM South-South politics, two essentially psychological variables—racial consciousness and nationalism— quickly emerge. The issue of race, for better or for worse, has long permeated the Caribbean; it was an integral element of the slave-based plantation societies imposed by European imperialism, and has continued to be an important aspect of the area's social fabric in the postcolonial period, one example being Trinidad and Tobago's affinity for ethnically driven politics revolving around its black and East Asian communities. In external affairs, one key way in which such sentiment has manifested itself is the strong emotive power that Africa wields over both West Indian elites and masses. Historically the North American and Western European links have tended to dominate the political and economic dimensions of the Caribbean's international panorama. Africa, however, has often reigned supreme in the cultural realm, as exemplified by the critical impact it has exerted on the region's intellectual dialog through the works of such ardent admirers as Marcus Garvey, George Padmore, and C.L.R. James.[16] Or, if one prefers a more grass-roots perspective, certainly the immense popularity of the music and the life-style associated with the Rastafarian Movement has functioned to intensity the general population's interest in their African roots, as well as generating an increased sense of solidarity with African nations and causes. Such Afrocentrism could, when seen against the backdrop of the need for CARICOM nations to expand their maneuvering room on the global stage, lend significant impetus to the creation of a much more ambitious South-South postdependency policy edifice.

Equally powerful is the appeal of nationalism. Defined here as the "manifestation by a stable community of a clear sense of group consciousness and a strong determination to acquire, retain, and reaffirm its separate, distinctive identity,"[17] nationalism has been and continues to be one of the most potent influences on modern political attitudes and behavior. Practically every society, regardless of its ideological or other idiosyncrasies, has proved susceptible to its lure. Standing at the very core of contemporary nationalistic sentiment is the principle of national self-determination—the idea that all peoples have an inalienable right to achieve and exercise theoretically total control over their political, socioeconomic, and cultural destinies. In its most elementary sense, therefore, nationalism represents the universal desire for freedom from any kind of external domination, or, to use postdependency terminology, for full and effective sovereignty. Initially such feelings expressed themselves most forcefully in the form of anticolonialism, but today they are most likely to be galvanized by fears of neoimperialism and dependency.

Radical dependencia theorists are, of course, highly skeptical about nationalism's counterdependency potential, their basic premise being that under normal (i.e., nonrevolutionary) conditions the local political arena will be dominated by the comprador class, which benefits exorbitantly from the dependent status quo and thus has no incentive to mobilize the masses to challenge it. In other words, says Cal Clark, they are convinced that, once the center-periphery relationship is firmly in place, the battle against it must move far outside a society's conventional parameters because at this point the metropole has so thoroughly penetrated "the indigenous leadership by entering into a coalition with a narrow and privileged elite class [that] this elite [will] adjure any structural or bargaining advantages that might accrue to the dependent state because an erosion in external dependence would undermine its own privileged position."[18] When, however, the seeds of destruction phenomenon (discussed in Chapter 1) is factored into the equation, it becomes much more feasible to suggest that at least some important segments of a peripheral establishment may be engulfed by the nationalistic currents swirling around them and swept into the vortex of counterdependency struggles. Survey research undertaken by William Biddle and John Stephens on the attitudes of Jamaica's elites in the 1970s seems to support this hypothesis, for they found that even the island's normally pro-western or pro–United States capitalists had begun to display greater enthusiasm for independent foreign and domestic policies as dependency's political-economic liabilities became more apparent.[19]

It should not be too surprising, given the generally moderate, mainstream dynamics of West Indian politics, to find most nationalistic CARICOM leaders fitting more comfortably into a pragmatic than a radical mold. Consequently their counterdependency impulses are not likely to be externalized in grandiose gestures such as wholesale expropriation of foreign investors' assets (à la the Cuban Revolution), but rather in efforts to maneuver themselves into a position of enhanced negotiating strength. Within this less confrontational context a South-South strategy could be seen as a very attractive (i.e., moderate or pragmatic) means to make the transition to the controlled dependence stage of the postdependency continuum.

Inhibiting Factors

The demise of strategic/military bipolarity emerges as a double-edged sword at the systemic level of analysis, appearing in both the asset and liability columns of the viability balance sheet. It definitely could, as noted previously, have the salutory effect of opening up more political space for the LDCs by engendering an international climate wherein the superpowers should be less inclined to try to maintain tight control over certain regions or countries. However, as is often the case, there can also be a downside involved.

The Cold War that flowed from post–World War II bipolarity did not totally immobilize the LDCs. To the contrary, it presented some splendid opportunities for them—collectively as well as individually—to capitalize on the desire of the Soviets and the Americans to draw as many countries as possible into their respective orbits. What lent special urgency to this exercise was the prevailing zero-sum mentality in both camps that led them to perceive any gain by their opponent, no matter how marginal, as a major setback that (in a worst-case scenario) threatened to tip the balance of global power decisively against them. Such paranoia could often be manipulated quite easily by developing nations, the classic ploy being to try to lure the two antagonists into a bidding frenzy for one's loyalties. Although this strategy was usually employed most successfully by LDCs operating alone, it could be multilateralized. Certainly an important, if not publicly stated, concern of the Nonaligned Movement has been to provide a mechanism for Third World countries to coordinate their efforts to take advantage of the East-West rivalry in order to advance their own interests on the international stage.

Such opportunities have, however, largely faded along with the Cold War. Moscow and Washington are no longer engaged in a global quest for allies in order to enforce or to break out of containment. Indeed the Soviet bloc no longer exists, its final death knell having sounded in July 1991 when the Warsaw Pact was formally disbanded. The LDCs, like the rest of the international community, were grateful that the U.S.–Soviet tensions that had too long endangered world peace and perhaps even human survival had subsided. Yet such euphoria inevitably has to be tempered by the realization that these developments have seriously undermined the Third World's political and strategic importance as far as the two traditional superpowers are concerned, which in turn suggests that it will no longer be feasible to pit them against one another and thereby gain such developmental benefits as trade concessions and aid. In effect, then, the South-South option has become more difficult for the LDCs to pursue, since their bargaining power has been diminished by the fact that they no longer possess some key Cold War blue chips to lay on the postdependency negotiating table.

Certain dynamics in the economic sphere, which became increasingly apparent in the 1980s, constitute another systemic variable whose impact on the LDC quest for controlled dependence may in some respects be quite dysfunctional. However, unlike the demise of Cold War bipolarity, which is likely to be a rather durable feature of the international political order, economic conditions tend to be more susceptible to change and therefore may mount somewhat less formidable obstacles to the postdependency aspirations of the CARICOM and other developing nations.

In any case, the general contours of the problem currently confronting the LDCs can be summarized quite easily: the overall pattern of global commerce has undergone alterations that have eroded the relative importance of the developing nations vis-à-vis the world's industrialized power centers. The trade figures in Table 4.3, which can be seen as an indication of U.S. priorities regarding its economic partners, illustrate this phenomenon. What has been occurring, in other words, is that the developed countries have been devoting proportionately more attention to North-North than to North-South commerce. Such figures can, of course, sometimes be deceiving. For instance, most basic commodity prices dropped in the 1980s, which suggests that at least some of the decline in the aggregate dollar value of African and Middle Eastern exports to the United States can be attributed to such financial considerations rather than reductions in the volume of trade. If this were the total extent of the matter, it could be seen as a temporary anomaly related to oversupply (and hence lower prices).

Table 4.3 U.S. Trade with Selected Regions, 1980–1988

	Percentage Increase in Exports to	Percentage Increase in Imports from
Western Europe	23.3	119.5
Canada	95.6	96.4
Japan	81.5	203.5
Latin America	11.2	71.5
Africa	−18.0	−60.7
Middle East	− 8.8	−27.8

Source: Calculated from annual U.S. dollar volume, from data in *World Almanac* (New York: Pharos Books, 1990), p. 133.

More ominous, however, is the very real possibility that such trade patterns are symptomatic of the emergence of postindustrial societies in the North whose economies revolve much more around the high-tech and service sectors than heavy manufacturing.[20] Such a transformation could permanently reduce the demand for the raw materials that have traditionally been the mainstay of Third World exports, which in turn would imply that the bargaining power of the LDCs in any North-South negotiations would be undermined because the economic health of the metropoles would not be as dependent as was previously the case on assured access to the developing nations' natural resources. A similar line of reasoning could be applied to the U.S. export figures in Table 4.3, the key idea being that the significance of the LDCs as consumers of U.S. goods seems to be diminishing, and consequently it may become more difficult for them to extract trade and aid concessions as a quid pro quo for guaranteed entry to their domestic markets.

It would, of course, be a gross exaggeration to suggest that the developed nations are likely any time in the foreseeable future to become totally free of reliance on strategic raw materials imported from the Third World. Yet the postindustrial form of global interdependence that now seems to be emerging, which might be described as "metrocentric" in the sense that North-North economic relations appear to be its most dynamic element, could very well prove to be somewhat inhospitable to the pursuit of South-South postdependency politics.

Beyond such systemic obstacles, there are several factors that can hinder initiatives aimed at achieving controlled dependence that are multi-dimensional in the sense that they operate across levels of analysis. Specifically, they span the LDC subsystemic and the West Indian categories. The two key areas of concern here involve: (1) centrifugal tendencies detrimental to the overall consolidation of South-South solidarity and having in particular the potential to foster disunity within LDC negotiating blocs (e.g., the Group of 77 or CARICOM); and (2) the development by Third World governments of a quick-fix mentality that manifests itself in a preference for bilateral North-South arrangements rather than a multilateral South-South approach when dealing with the industrialized nations.

Factors Promoting Centrifugal Tendencies

The two variables mentioned most frequently within the context of centrifugal forces are the differential levels of development within the Third World and the closely related question of assuring equitable distribution of any benefits emerging from the collective bargaining process. Extreme care, says Fidel Castro, must be taken to assure that "cooperation among underdeveloped countries [recognizes] the heterogeneity of the Third World in regard to underdevelopment levels, with a view to preventing a few countries with a certain level of industrialization and exporting capability from reaping most of the benefits."[21] Certainly CARICOM has not been immune to such debilitating forces, as evidenced by the formation of the Organization of Eastern Caribbean States (OECS, discussed further below).

Central to this complex panorama is the very simple but often

overlooked fact that the Third World is diverse. Falling within its purview
are countries whose populations range from 100,000 (or even less) to
hundreds of millions, whose size varies from small islands that are literally
dots on the map to such territorial behemoths as India and China, and whose
natural resources span a spectrum entailing virtual treasure troves at one
extreme to practically bare shelves at the other. Prompted by this diversity,
some international relations specialists have rejected the term *Third World* as
a generic label for the developing nations, preferring to add to the roster such
concepts as NICs as well as fourth and even fifth worlds.[22] The World Bank,
for instance, subdivides the LDCs into four categories based on their gross
national product (GNP)—low-income countries (approximately fifty);
middle-income countries that are oil importers (approximately forty);
middle-income countries that are petroleum exporters (approximately
fifteen); and high-income countries that are petroleum exporters
(approximately six).

But whatever categorization schemes might be employed, the same
fundamental rule applies that differential levels of modernization or
development tend to generate idiosyncratic perceptions of interest within any
LDC collectivity, which in turn can transform what one might expect to be a
fairly orderly North-South bargaining exercise into a political quagmire.
Theoretically, according to an idealized South-South scenario, the
developing nations involved will coalesce smoothly into a united front and
then should, given the enhanced strength that normally comes from
combined numbers, be able to deal much more effectively with their
antagonists than otherwise would be the case. In practice, however,
negotiating priorities must be established before the formal talks begin. It is
at this point that the Third World team may experience serious internal
dissension, for its individual members will probably demand that the needs
associated with their particular level of development be endorsed as being
the most important. For example, countries with some manufacturing
capacity could want the group's pooled bargaining power to be applied first
to acquiring trade concessions for finished products, while those whose
economies are still mainly agrarian might insist that commodity exports
receive primary consideration. Similar confrontations could occur over the
procurement of developmental aid, with the more economically advanced
nations emphasizing such agenda items as sophisticated technology transfers,
and those on a more rudimentary plane being in all likelihood more
interested in getting assistance for infrastructure projects. To the extent that
such bickering may occur, it would simply confirm that the South-South
strategy is vulnerable to a fairly common phenomenon in international
affairs—the proclivity for governments to use their influence to try to have
the general good defined in terms of their parochial national concerns. The
result, of course, is disunity as the formulating of a common negotiating

position becomes dominated by the clash rather than the harmonization of interests.

Equally divisive can be the necessity for the Third World to reach agreement on guidelines and mechanisms to distribute equitably any benefits achieved by its exercise of collective bargaining power. Here again the fault lines tend to flow from developmental imbalances, with the smaller and weaker nations often wanting guarantees of distributive justice prior to any negotiations with the North because they fully realize that a laissez-faire approach could very well mean that they might fall further behind their fellows in the quest for material progress and effective sovereignty.

The logic involved here is quite similar to that which led the NAM and other Third World representatives to call for a new international economic order. These demands were grounded in the overwhelming body of evidence gathered in the 1960s and 1970s that showed that, even when the LDCs were experiencing growth, the gap between the globe's rich and poor states could actually be increasing. The explanation for this exasperating state of affairs lies in the markedly different starting points for the parties involved. Using a hypothetical situation where the GNP index of developed country A is 1,000 and that of Third World nation X is 500, a little simple arithmetic will demonstrate how X can have the higher growth rate and yet still lose ground to A:

A's	1,000 x	8% (annual growth rate) =	1,080
X's	500 x	10% (annual growth rate) =	550

The development gap has moved from 500 index points to 530. Following the same formula, the difference would rise to 561 points in the second year and 590 points in the third year, which would represent an 18 percent erosion in X's original GNP position vis-à-vis A.

The same principle holds when dealing with a group of LDCs in which there are substantial developmental differentials. Without some compensatory modalities (call it affirmative action, if you wish) to regulate the flow of benefits in order to create conditions conducive to significant progress toward a more balanced configuration, the chasm between the have-littles and the have-nothings will simply persist and perhaps even enlarge. Certainly this appears to be the case historically, as the twenty-five-year average growth rates for various classes of developing countries in Table 4.4 indicate. The dilemma, of course, is that it can be just as difficult to achieve equity understandings within the context of Third World relations as it has been to bring about a new North-South economic order. To fail to find a remedy, however, runs the risk of creating a heightened sense of relative deprivation and frustration that, say many observers, can easily lead to escalating tensions and perhaps ultimately violence.[23] But even

Table 4.4 GNP per Capita and Its Growth Rate, by Income Groups, 1950–1975

	Population, 1975 (in Millions)	Dollars, 1975	Growth Rate of GNP per Capita[a] (Percentage per Year)
Lower-income countries	1,146	265	1.1
Middle-income countries[b]	1,118	266–520	3.7
Upper-middle-income countries	370	521–1,075	3.4
Higher-income countries	100	1,076+	5.2
Developing countries[c]	2,732		3.4

Source: Compiled from preliminary and unpublished World Bank data, and reprinted with permission from Roger D. Hansen, *The North/South Stalemate* (New York: McGraw-Hill, 1979), p. 95.

[a]In 1974 dollars.

[b]If China is excluded, middle-income countries' population equals 298 million, growth rate equals 2.4 percent.

[c]If China is excluded, developing countries' population equals 1,912 million, growth rate equals 3.0 percent.

discounting the apocalyptic possibilities, it is obvious that such a psychological climate would not be very amenable to South-South postdependency politics.

The broader the participatory range of Third World cooperation and hence, at least theoretically, the greater the bargaining power available to make and consolidate the transition to dependence, the more complex and less susceptible to solution these problems arising from developmental imbalances are likely to become. Thus one is confronted with the irony that increasing the operational scope of the South-South option may in reality function as a disincentive rather than an inducement for some countries, especially those that are small and less modernized, to embrace it as a viable counterdependency strategy.

These centrifugal tendencies have long plagued the Latin American scene. A typical pattern, says Elizabeth Ferris, finds the more developed Hispanic nations

> most likely to support those Third World demands which will enable them to emulate First World economic progress. However, their support of Third World causes is pragmatic; they support those measures which will increase their access to the rewards of the international capitalist system, but they do not support the restructuring of that system to enable all Third World countries to share in the wealth. Traditionally, [such nations] have not been supportive of Latin American integration schemes or other attempts to forge unified Latin American bargaining positions.[24]

In other instances, countries have become so impatient with what they have perceived to be the slow progress of existing hemispheric vehicles in addressing their concerns that they have experimented with scaling down the geographical scope of their cooperation programs, as illustrated by the formation of the Andean Group in 1969 by some disgruntled members of the Latin American Free Trade Association.[25]

Similar fragmentation has occurred in the West Indies.[26] In 1981 several of CARICOM's smaller participants, complaining that their rewards from the association's common market arrangements were insufficient, formed a parallel group known as the Organization of Eastern Caribbean States in order to service their distinctive developmental needs.[27] The OECS is in many respects a miniaturized version of CARICOM. For example, it also seeks to promote intraregional free trade—its institutional mechanism being the ECCM—and to facilitate foreign policy coordination, especially with respect to Caribbean Basin affairs. Normally, however, it would not assume the role of a high-profile bargaining agent in North-South negotiations, its members generally preferring to continue to handle such matters through CARICOM.

The disaggregative impact of the OECS was graphically demonstrated in 1983 when its members, along with Jamaica and Barbados, flouted the CARICOM principle of a united front on crucial regional and international issues by enthusiastically collaborating in the U.S. invasion of Grenada. In the process, says Anthony Payne,

> the damage done . . . to Caribbean integration was enormous. It was, after all, not only that the region disagreed over what to do in Grenada, . . . but that the "invading states" deliberately connived to conceal their intentions from their remaining CARICOM partners—Trinidad, Guyana, Belize, and the Bahamas. Understandably the other leaders, especially [Trinidad's] George Chambers and Forbes Burnham, the president of Guyana, felt that they had been made to look foolish.[28]

The often vicious quarreling that ensued carried over into the United Nations, where, when a resolution condemning the assault was submitted to the General Assembly, Trinidad and Tobago, Guyana, the Bahamas, and Grenada voted with the majority in supporting it, while Barbados, Jamaica, Antigua and Barbuda, Dominica, St. Lucia, and St. Vincent were opposed. Belize abstained and St. Kitts–Nevis was absent.[29] While this incident revolved around ideological and security questions rather than the economic issues that usually dominate the postdependency dialog, it illustrates the political animosities that can have a negative spillover effect into other dimensions of South-South relations, poisoning the general atmosphere and thereby making any kind of collaboration more difficult.

Factors Promoting a Quick-Fix Mentality

Rivaling centrifugal tendencies as an obstacle to South-South postdependency politics is the propensity for LDCs to embrace bilateral arrangements with an industrialized country in order to resolve their most urgent economic problems. Such behavior stems mainly from the fact that public officials often do not perceive that they have the luxury of more protracted scenarios such as the South-South option for dealing with their dilemmas, being instead susceptible to a mind-set (which might sarcastically be called the magic bullet syndrome) that focuses their attention almost exclusively on finding an instantaneous solution for whatever policy conflagration happens to be erupting at the moment. Thus when confronted with developmental difficulties, such crisis managers, whose conceptual frameworks consist of short-term tactics rather than long-term strategies, are understandably prone to succumb to the temptation to turn to the most lucrative source of fast assistance—the modernized nations or the financial institutions they control such as the World Bank and the International Monetary Fund. The massive Third World debt stands as graphic testimony to the willingness of southern governments to make, either figuratively or literally, pilgrimages to the North. Unfortunately, the end result is seldom salvation, but rather increased vulnerability to external penetration and control.

While this quick-fix mentality and its corollary bilateralism can, as indicated above, evolve as an independent variable with no connection whatsoever to Third World centrifugal forces, the two phenomena are in fact often intimately related. Specifically, the greater the fragmentary pressures on LDCs that serve to complicate their collective bargaining initiatives and hence probably postpone the day when benefits become available, the greater the likelihood that some of them, driven by the conviction that immediate remedial action on the developmental front is imperative, will strike out on their own in an attempt to secure individual North-South accords.

Once a special link is firmly established, an LDC may be reluctant to abandon the perceived security involved for the uncharted waters of South-South postdependency politics. Certainly, according to John Ravenhill, such calculations have affected the sentiments of some Third World governments about the Lomé process in the sense that,

> for individual ACP states, the danger of the collective approach was that their traditional patron would feel less of an obligation toward safeguarding their interests once the obligations of the patron had been diluted by being collectivized to the [European] Community as a whole. Accordingly, ACP states continued to attempt to exploit their traditional bilateral ties with individual Community member states to obtain particularistic concessions for themselves.[30]

A related concern could arise with respect to an LDC's freedom of action. Although the South-South model promises to expand a nation's political space, some states may see it as actually limiting their options by demanding that they pursue a common bargaining agenda in concert with other Third World states. To do so could mean that a particular country would have to forgo courses of action that it could otherwise pursue as an independent actor and might not be able to strike immediately in capitalizing on whatever developmental opportunities might arise. These attitudes are similar to those displayed by senators who opposed (successfully) U.S. membership in the League of Nations, the basic argument at the time being that entry would undermine the United States' sovereignty, since its ability to act unilaterally in world affairs would be compromised by its obligation to observe League standards of international conduct. From such a perspective, then, the rugged individualism of a bilateral approach to North-South relations appears much more attractive than South-South multilateralism.

It is, of course, perfectly feasible that bilateralism could serve as the means to make the transition to controlled dependence via the superclient, Singapore, or some other scenario, and even beyond into the realm of acquired structural power (i.e., the protointerdependence stage on the postdependency continuum [see Chapter 2]). But what is possible may not be what is preferable from the standpoint of the most ambitious advocates of counterdependency initiatives.

Bilateralism's basic shortcoming, insist its critics, is that its horizons are much too narrow. Specifically, they contend that what it offers is at most status adjustment to balanced interdependence for a relatively few Third World countries, not structural transformation of the international system. This conclusion is predicated on the assumption that it is extremely dubious that the number of individual success stories would ever be sufficient to have the cumulative impact of producing a comprehensive new global order wherein the developing nations would find that the serious vulnerabilities that traditionally exposed them to foreign domination have for the most part been eliminated and replaced by a network of positive sensitivities entailing significant benefits for both Third World and industrialized states. In short, bilateralism becomes equated with the sirens of Greek mythology, diverting those trying to make the passage to the highest level of postdependency politics and its rewards into a disastrous dead end.

On a more pragmatic note, another obstacle to effective collective bargaining on the Third World's part is its lack of a sophisticated capacity for empirical economic research on a global scale. Knowledge, it has long been recognized, is power. It is for this reason that espionage is commonly described as the world's second-oldest profession and that huge information-gathering establishments are an integral part of modern governments. Traditionally the mandate of these national intelligence communities has been defined mainly in military and security terms. In the modern era, however, economic data is often considered an equally important asset in international affairs. Thus the industrialized world maintains state-of-the-art systems for procuring and processing such information. Indeed the private sector in the developed states has also become active in this field, some companies even going so far as to launch elaborate covert corporate espionage operations.[31]

The LDCs, on the other hand, are sorely lacking in such capabilities. They are, in effect, being outgunned in the data wars and, consequently, frequently find themselves at a distinct disadvantage in North-South negotiations. It has not, for instance, been unusual for the ACP representatives in the Lomé process to rely heavily on their EC counterparts to provide statistical raw material crucial to the discussions. This hardly represents, to say the least, optimal conditions under which to conduct business central to the Third World's economic future, for within such an environment it is almost inevitable that the LDCs' role will be reactive rather than proactive. They will, in other words, probably find it very difficult to seize the initiative because they lack the hard data necessary to support their case and hence have to be content to respond to proposals coming from the industrialized countries. This is not the assertive bargaining scenario envisioned by the South-South paradigm. It is, instead, more likely to become an exercise in polite diplomatic dancing on the Third World's part that will not be particularly conducive to the rapid advance of the collective postdependency cause.

One final cautionary note, regarding the prospects for close CARICOM postdependency collaboration with Africa, needs to be sounded. While there is, as discussed previously, a strong cultural and psychological affinity between the two regions, there likewise are some potential countervailing elements that must be factored into the equation. Certainly some serious questions have been raised about the extent to which Africa presents a viable option for diversifying West Indian trade. One problem arises in conjunction with what might be called complementary comparative advantage, which when applied in a rudimentary dyadic situation simply means that each party will be highly efficient in supplying the products needed by the other and therefore both will profit significantly from the relationship. An ideal hypothetical case would see Africa exporting items A, B, C and importing X, Y, Z, while the West Indies export X, Y, Z and import A, B, C. But in reality the profiles of African and Caribbean exports are in many respects quite similar, especially when we focus on primary commodity goods. Both areas are major producers of sugar, tropical fruits, and the like. In effect, then, both are exporting items M, N, O and thus lack the synergy necessary to maintain high levels of commerce. Moreover, even when there is favorable supply-demand configuration, transportation costs can be so prohibitive as to render it irrelevant.[32] The CARICOM-African arena, then, does not appear to be a particularly fertile ground for trying to operationalize the positive correlation that is often said to exist between mutually beneficial economic exchanges and cooperation in the broader political sphere.

Also, with respect to the ACP Group, there may be some latent concern among its CARICOM members regarding the possibility that they could find themselves permanently subordinate to its numerically superior African contingent. In the past, strong Caribbean representation within the upper echelons of the ACP Secretariat has served to compensate for this larger imbalance. In 1990, however, Edward Carrington, a West Indian who had long served as the organization's chief representative in Brussels to the EC, was replaced by an African. Such rotations are, of course, quite common in geographically diverse associations, the idea being to avoid even the slightest hint of insensitivity to any particular region. Selection of the site for the NAM's triennial summit has, for example, always been very much affected by such considerations because the host nation's chief executive automatically becomes the Movement's leader until the next conclave. Nevertheless, the Carrington case could be seen as symbolizing the precariousness of CARICOM's influence within the ACP coalition and its vulnerability to being unwillingly relegated to the role of junior partner. If so, West Indian enthusiasm for South-South postdependency initiatives that include a large African component could suffer.

Weighing the Factors

Any government pondering the question of becoming heavily committed to South-South postdependency politics faces a daunting task because, as the preceding material indicates, it is extremely difficult to determine in which direction the scales are tipping. Do they suggest that such a strategy in pursuit of North-South bargaining power and controlled dependence is viable? Small states such as those in the West Indies must be especially careful in weighing and evaluating all the factors involved, for their resource limitations (both human and otherwise) allow very little room for error in setting their foreign policy priorities. Indeed it could very well require years for a Caribbean government just to recoup from a serious miscalculation, years that should have been devoted to real progress toward its modernization goals. What conclusions, then, can be reached concerning the feasibility of the South-South option for the CARICOM nations?

Certainly the negative impact of centrifugal forces and the bilateral quick-fix mentality cannot be overestimated. The littered trail of failed attempts at macroregional or functional integration, especially in the Western

Hemisphere, stands as tragic evidence of their disaggregative powers. Among the victims in the Caribbean is the West Indies Federation (1958–1962), which in many respects can be seen as a classic case study of inability to conquer the problems posed by differential levels of development within an organization and by demands coming from smaller members for assurances that benefits will be distributed equitably.

It would be extremely naive to assume that these issues can somehow be ignored, for the harsh reality is that they are an integral component of the South-South postdependency landscape. The dynamics of the process will, therefore, inexorably draw them into the picture, thereby creating the real danger that their highly disruptive potential will be realized.

Imaginative and pragmatic leaders capable of making quick compensatory adjustments can act as an intervening variable, ameliorating things somewhat by bringing to bear their crisis-management and damage-control skills. But such a response, no matter how finely honed or deftly executed, is fundamentally flawed because it is, to use a medical analogy, essentially oriented toward relieving the pain rather than curing the disease. Thus the respite provided is likely to be ephemeral, for the pressures associated with centrifugal forces and quick-fix bilateralism will continue to build and almost surely will finally reach the point where they exceed anyone's ability to contain them. The people chosen to head the West Indies Federation, for example, were among the Caribbean's best and brightest, yet they were not able to save it.

At this juncture it would appear inadvisable to recommend the South-South postdependency option to the CARICOM states, for the pessimistic scenario painted above suggests that ultimately the centrifugal and bilateral tendencies will prove to be insurmountable obstacles. The key, however, as to whether these dysfunctional factors can be neutralized and overcome lies not in such intervening variables as leadership attributes, but instead is to be found in the larger context within which South-South politics is to be pursued. To the extent that this environment is, to use modern computer terminology, "user friendly," the possibly paralytic elements of the equation are likely to become increasingly less significant. In a sense, then, it could be said that the structural characteristics of such an environment endow it with the functional equivalent of an immune system, allowing it to tolerate what otherwise would be debilitating antipostdependency viruses and to continue to operate effectively despite their presence. Such key contextual antibodies relevant to CARICOM's situation can be found at both the macrosystemic and hemispheric subsystemic levels of analysis.

The bipolar configuration, whether tight or somewhat more flexible, that the international system displayed throughout most of the post–World War II era was not warmly hospitable to the cultivation of effective sovereignty by the West Indies. Unlike some other LDCs that were able to capitalize on

U.S.–Soviet Cold War rivalries to acquire large sums of developmental aid and a degree of influence on the international stage due to the superpowers' ardor in courting them, the CARICOM nations fell victim to the classical politics of great power spheres of influence. Just as the Kremlin would not tolerate any challenges to its authority in areas it considered vital to its security (as epitomized by its 1956 Hungarian and 1968 Czechoslovakian interventions), so also was Washington determined to secure its southern borders by maintaining a tight grip over Caribbean Basin affairs. Among its more spectacular and controversial attempts to rid the region of what it considered to be undesirable political and ideological elements were the 1954 CIA–orchestrated overthrow of the Arbenz government in Guatemala and John Kennedy's 1961 Bay of Pigs fiasco in Cuba. The 1983 invasion of Grenada exemplifies the most blatant application of such strong-arm tactics in the West Indies.

The Reagan administration was from the very beginning hostile to Maurice Bishop's New Jewel Revolution in Grenada, a main catalyst for this belligerence being St. George's stubbornly independent nonaligned foreign policy that included a particular relationship almost guaranteed to trigger Washington's paranoia—very close ties to Castro's Cuba. The White House, infuriated with such heresy, accused Bishop of having become a Soviet-Cuban puppet who was turning the island into a Communist bastion that threatened its neighbors and served as a major conduit for eastern bloc arms to Central American guerrillas. In early October 1983 a schism in the New Jewel Movement led to Bishop's overthrow. A rather chaotic period followed during which numerous civilians were killed or wounded when the army opened fire on a mass demonstration protesting the coup, Bishop and several of his cabinet members were summarily executed, and martial law (which included provisions for shooting anyone who violated curfew regulations) was declared. At this point, the OECS decided that the deteriorating situation represented such a danger to its members that intervention was necessary and invited the United States to participate. Reagan, who had already been thinking and planning along these lines, readily agreed, and on October 25, 1983, an invasion was launched by the United States, four OECS nations (Antigua and Barbuda, Dominica, St. Lucia, and St. Vincent), Jamaica, and Barbados. The Pentagon quickly took control of the operation, its Caribbean collaborators supplying only a token contingent of three hundred to four hundred men to an expeditionary force that totaled about fifteen thousand troops on land and sea. Despite fierce resistance from some of the approximately 750 Cubans who were in Grenada working on various aid projects, the island was firmly secured on November 1, 1983. This attack not only terminated Grenada's experimental foray into effective sovereignty, but in a larger sense it also constituted the final step in incorporating the West Indies into the Caribbean–Central American tradition of U.S. Marines storming ashore to dispose of governments that are not to Washington's liking.[33]

Circumstances that served to constrict the political space available to the CARICOM states were, however, soon overshadowed by the watershed events of the late 1980s and early 1990s (especially in Eastern Europe) that verified that the disintegration of the bipolar Cold War system, which had been under way for some time, was now complete. The result, as far as the West Indies were concerned, was a new international playing field with a much less rigid military and security power structure that afforded them a better chance to begin to take control of their own destinies.

Recognize, however, that simply because such opportunities for more independent political action on the global stage exist does not necessarily mean that they will be quickly seized. But interject a strong survival incentive and the odds increase markedly. The growing economic integration of the developed nations constitutes such a stimulus. Not only are Third World countermeasures to this trend imperative, but reason as well as sheer expediency practically dictates that they must be multilateral because few LDCs have the capability to mount an effective individual response.

It is this mutually reinforcing combination of systemic transfigurations that has produced a global environment not only conducive to, but in certain respects almost requiring, collective action by the developing countries. In other words, then, it is not simply a matter of the CARICOM nations choosing to pursue the South-South postdependency opportunities the demise of Cold War bipolarity presents. Instead, economic survival as well as any significant probability of generating some immunity to dependency's ravages (i.e., acquiring effective economic sovereignty) may very well demand that these prospects be seriously investigated.

At the subsystemic level of analysis it appears that the Latin American community in general and some key players in particular—especially Venezuela—are more attuned than ever before to the idea of establishing cooperative ties with the Caribbean in order to maximize hemispheric unity. Admittedly such pan-American aspirations often have not translated into significant progress in the past, the basic problem being that despite constant rhetorical support for the principle, serious interest in actually implementing programs has tended to wax and wane greatly. Pessimists, therefore, might conclude that whatever current enthusiasm exists is but another phase in the historical cycle that will, like its predecessors, fade without anything important having been accomplished.

Such cynicism may prove to be warranted. On the other hand, Latin America, like other developing areas, cannot ignore or escape the consequences of the movement toward economic megablocs in the industrialized world. In particular, the proposed North American Free Trade Area (NAFTA) has aroused intense concern.[34] Thus hemispheric solidarity assumes unprecedented urgency given the perceived need to enhance collective North-South bargaining power, especially vis-à-vis the United States. Incorporating CARICOM into this scenario not only makes conceptual sense, but also the West Indies would bring with them some substantial political assets in terms of their existing special relationships with the EC through the Lomé accords and with the United States through the CBI. Thus, as was the case at the global level, a number of factors have converged to create a Latin American environment quite hospitable to the pursuit of South-South postdependency politics on CARICOM's part.

To the extent that this hemispheric dimension to CARICOM's South-South agenda developed, it would give the West Indies the distinction of being the Third World region with perhaps the most extensive network of connections dedicated to the acquisition and exercise of bargaining power within the context of North-South politics. Specifically, CARICOM would be linked to the EC, Africa, and the Pacific Basin through the Lomé channel, to the United States through the CBI, and to North and South America though the dynamics surrounding the NAFTA process. Consequently, in contrast to the tribulations that have too often in the past been inflicted on the Caribbean as the result of its location as a crossroads between Europe, North America, and Latin America, that status currently puts the West Indies in a unique and apparently favorable position to explore the South-South strategy.

Overall, then, it seems that the feasibility analysis with regard to South-South initiatives by the CARICOM states is positive. There are, of course, no guarantees that the West Indies will succeed in making the initial transition to controlled dependence, but the general indicators suggest that it is indeed a policy option meriting serious consideration.

Notes

1. See, e.g., J. David Singer's seminal article on this topic, "The Level-of-Analysis Problem in International Relations," in James N. Rosenau, ed., *International Politics and Foreign Policy* (New York: Free Press, 1969), pp. 20–29.

2. One classical formulation of systems theory in general and the various permutations the international system can assume is in Morton A. Kaplan, *System and Process in International Politics* (New York: John Wiley and Sons, 1957). In ch. 2 he suggests a typology encompassing six distinct forms of the international system: balance of power; loose bipolar; tight bipolar; universal; hierarchical (which can be subdivided into directive and nondirective varieties); and unit veto.

The term *multipolarity,* at least as used here, corresponds most closely to Kaplan's balance of power system, the main difference being that his conceptualization tends to place more emphasis on military than pure economic capabilities.

3. Among Washington's most blatant—as well as effective—attempts to

neutralize strong Caribbean exponents of nonalignment and ideological pluralism were the counteroffensives that it mounted against Cheddi Jagan of Guyana (1970s) and Maurice Bishop of Grenada (1980s).

4. Desmond Hoyte, "Making the Quantum Leap: Imperatives, Opportunities, and Challenges for CARICOM," *Caribbean Affairs* 2, no. 2 (April–June 1989): 55–56.

5. Andrés Serbín, "The CARICOM States and the Group of Three: A New Partnership Between Latin America and the Non-Hispanic Caribbean?" (paper presented at the sixteenth International Congress of the Latin American Studies Association, Washington, DC, April 4–6, 1991), pp. 8–9.

6. John Martz, "Ideology and Oil in the Circum-Caribbean," in H. Michael Erisman and John Martz, eds., *Colossus Challenged: The Struggle for Caribbean Influence* (Boulder, CO: Westview Press, 1982), p. 129.

7. Information concerning the Latin American linkages of the smaller CARICOM countries can be found in Jacqueline Braveboy-Wagner, "Caribbean Foreign Relations: Current State and Prospects for Diversification" (paper presented at the sixteenth International Congress of the Latin American Studies Association, Washington, DC, April 4–6, 1991), pp. 13–14.

8. For an overview of the evolving Latin American–Caribbean connection, see Andrés Serbín, "The Caribbean: Myths and Realities for the 1990s," *Journal of Interamerican Studies and World Affairs* 32, no. 2 (Summer 1990): 121–141.

9. See *Caribbean Update* (July 1990), p. 11, and *Caribbean Update* (October 1990), p. 11.

10. See *Caribbean Update* (July 1990), p. 12.

11. This dispute flared into violence in 1989 when the Venezuelan armed forces fired on a Trinidadian fishing boat they said was violating their territorial waters, and killed its captain. For details of this incident and a general analysis of the problem, see Anselm Francis, "The Gulf of Paria: Area of Conflict," *Caribbean Affairs* 3, no. 1 (January–March 1990): 26–37.

12. The Caribbean Basin, as defined by the CBI, encompassed Central America, Panama, and all the independent islands plus CARICOM'S two mainland members—Guyana and Belize. In practice, however, CBI eligibility was denied on ideological grounds to Castro's Cuba, revolutionary Grenada, and Sandinista Nicaragua.

13. For an excellent brief analysis, see Carmen Diana Deere, "A CBI Report Card," *Hemisphere* 3, no. 1 (Fall 1990): 29–31.

14. David Lewis, "Political Hegemony and Economic Crisis: The Challenges for U.S. Foreign Policy in the Caribbean" (paper presented at the sixteenth International Congress of the Latin American Studies Association, Washington, DC, April 4–6, 1991), pp. 11–12. A similar conclusion can be found in "CBI Fails to Boost Regional Exports," *Latin American Regional Reports: Caribbean Report* (June 20, 1991), p. 7, where it is stated that "comparing estimated total US imports in 1983 with the figures for the 12-month period ending September 1990, the Commerce Department has recorded a 36% decline for 18 Caribbean countries as a group." The only major bright spots were U.S. imports of textiles, clothing, and various nontraditional Caribbean products, which increased 106 percent from 1983 to September 1990.

15. This information, including the tables (4.1 and 4.2) from U.S. Department of Commerce and U.S. Department of State sources, can be found in Anthony P. González, "Recent Trends in International Economic Relations of the CARICOM States," *Journal of Interamerican Studies and World Affairs* 31, no. 3 (Fall 1989): 69.

16. For representative samples of their work, see Marcus Garvey, *Philosophy and Opinions of Marcus Garvey,* 2 vols. (New York: Arno Press, 1968–1969); C.L.R. James, *The Future in the Present: Selected Writings* (London: Allison and Busby,

1977); and George Padmore, *Pan-Africanism or Communism* (Garden City, NY: Doubleday, 1971).

17. For a good, concise discussion of nationalism's nature, development, and modern influence, see Hans Kohn, "Nationalism," *International Encyclopedia of the Social Sciences* (New York: Crowell Collier and Macmillan, 1968), pp. 63–70.

18. Cal Clark, "The Process of Dependence and Dependency Reversal" (paper presented at the International Studies Association conference, Los Angeles, March 20–22, 1980), p. 21.

19. See William J. Biddle and John D. Stephens, "Dependency and Foreign Policy: Theory and Practice in Jamaica" (paper presented at the Latin American Studies Association conference, Boston, October 23–25, 1986).

20. A recent discussion of the concept of a postindustrial society can be found in Fred L. Block, *Postindustrial Possibilities: A Critique of Economic Discourse* (Berkeley: University of California Press, 1990).

21. Fidel Castro, *The World Economic and Social Crisis* (Havana: Publishing Office of the Council of State, 1983), p. 160.

22. See, e.g., Hollis B. Chenery, "Restructuring the World Economy," *Foreign Affairs* 53 (January 1975): 258–263.

23. Two classic examples of theoretical works focusing on the relationship between relative deprivation and social violence are James C. Davies, "Toward a Theory of Revolution," *American Sociological Review* 27 (February 1962): 5–19; and Ted Robert Gurr, *Why Men Rebel* (Princeton, NJ: Princeton University Press, 1970).

24. Elizabeth G. Ferris, "Toward a Theory for the Comparative Analysis of Latin American Foreign Policy," in Elizabeth G. Ferris and Jennie K. Lincoln, eds., *Latin American Foreign Policies: Global and Regional Dimensions* (Boulder, CO: Westview Press, 1981), p. 247.

25. The charter members of the Andean Group were Bolivia, Colombia, Ecuador, Peru, and Venezuela.

26. Some general surveys of CARICOM that include good discussions of centrifugal tendencies in the organization can be found in Rosina Wiltshire, "Integration in Developing Regions as Competing Systems: CARICOM, the Caribbean Experiment," in Richard Millet and W. Marvin Will, eds., *The Restless Caribbean: Changing Patterns of International Relations* (New York: Praeger, 1979), pp. 251–265; Anthony Payne, "Whither CARICOM? The Performance and Prospects of Caribbean Integration in the 1980s," *International Journal* 40, no. 2 (Spring 1985): 207–228; and Anthony P. González, "Recent Trends," pp. 63–95.

27. The seven members of the OECS are Antigua and Barbuda, Dominica, Grenada, Montserrat, St. Kitts–Nevis, St. Lucia, and St. Vincent and the Grenadines. OECS members have not withdrawn from CARICOM. Rather, they remain affiliated with both institutions. Often the OECS, although a separate institutional entity, functions as a lobbying group for the smaller Caribbean islands within CARICOM.

28. Anthony Payne, "Whither CARICOM?" p. 222.

29. "CARICOM Division Over Grenada Given Emphasis," *Jamaica Daily Gleaner* (November 11, 1983). The overall vote on the resolution was 108 in favor to 9 against, with 27 abstentions.

30. John Ravenhill, *Collective Clientelism: The Lomé Conventions and North-South Relations* (New York: Columbia University Press, 1985), p. 44.

31. See Brian Freemantle, *The Steal: Counterfitting and Industrial Espionage* (London: M. Joseph, 1986); Joseph L. Cook and Earleen H. Cook, *Industrial Spying and Espionage* (Monticello, IL: Vance Bibliographies, 1985); and Jacques Bergier, *Secret Armies: The Growth of Corporate and Industrial Espionage* (Indianapolis, IN: Bobbs-Merrill, 1975).

32. These and other CARICOM diversification problems are discussed in Braveboy-Wagner, "Caribbean Foreign Relations," pp. 15–17.

33. More intense analysis of the militarizing of CARICOM politics is in H. Michael Erisman, "The CARICOM States and U.S. Foreign Policy: The Danger of Central Americanization," *Journal of Interamerican Studies and World Affairs* 31, no. 3 (Special Issue, Fall 1989): 141–182; and Alma Young and Dion Phillips, eds., *Militarization in the Non-Hispanic Caribbean* (Boulder, CO: Lynne Rienner Publishers, 1986).

34. For an excellent summary of NAFTA's evolution, the details of the proposed arrangement, and the potential problems it poses for the rest of the hemisphere, see "The New Gospel: North American Free Trade," *NACLA Report on the Americas* 24, no. 6 (May 1991): 9–38.

5

CARICOM and the Prospects
for Postdependency Politics

Some have called the 1980s the lost decade for the Third World. Certainly the litany of developmental calamities is in many instances far too long and much too depressing. Foreign debts soared, often to what seemed unmanageable proportions. Domestic economies were weak, with raging inflation and soaring unemployment and underemployment common. Indicators used to measure the general quality of life dropped precipitously, sometimes to the level of the 1960s or even the 1950s. Foreign aid, which normally could have helped to cushion the impact of such blows, became increasingly scarce. It is, therefore, understandable that many LDCs crossed the threshold into the 1990s with considerable foreboding.

Further complicating the current situation is the heavy pressure on Third World governments from both foreign and domestic sources to privatize their economies. Admittedly, some persuasive arguments can be made to support such demands, one popular and often accurate contention being that the efficiency of state-run enterprises tends to fall victim to a decisionmaking process dominated by political rather than business considerations. But too frequently overlooked in this infatuation with the supposed magic of the free market is the simple fact (which can be readily verified by a careful reading of the economic history of such industrial giants as the United States, Germany, and Japan) that government has a crucial role to play in the developmental drama. This can be particularly true in a Third World environment, where very limited human and natural resources may require the careful macroplanning and even macromanagement that only the state can provide. If, however, privatization is carried to an extreme, the public sector will lack the power to control the country's broad social dynamics and therefore will not be able to carry out its responsibilities (especially if they are defined not only as expanding the nation's GNP, but also as assuring a fairly equitable distribution of modernization's benefits). In short, just as excessive politicization or bureaucratization of production can undermine efficiency, so also can excessive privatization in an LDC deprive the government of the effective sovereignty it must have to make its necessary contribution to the developmental process. Particularly dangerous is the possibility that rampant privatization may render Third World countries extremely vulnerable to external penetration and domination. In other words, inherent in the privatization fetish of the 1990s is the real threat that it will in effect serve to disenfranchise LDCs economically and thereby revitalize the system of center-periphery dependency they have always found so abhorrent.

The West Indies have, as one might expect, shared in this general apprehension. In late 1989 Anthony Bryan warned that the Caribbean could find its external vulnerabilities adversely affected early in the 1990s by the outcomes of the negotiations for a 1990 revision and renewal of the Lomé Conventions; the Uruguay Round of General Agreement on Tariffs and Trade (GATT) discussions, also scheduled for completion in 1990; and the implementation by 1992 of the Single Europe Act. In each case, he said, the region's nations run the risk of seeing their trade and other economic preferences seriously eroded.[1] Also looming on the horizon is the challenge or, depending on one's viewpoint, the menace posed by the nascent NAFTA.[2]

CARICOM, motivated at least in part by its sensitivity to these potential problems, launched several initiatives aimed at strengthening its internal unity and, to a somewhat lesser extent, broadening its participatory scope. The key document in this process was the "Grand Anse Declaration and Work Programme for the Advancement of the Integration Movement," which was proclaimed by the West Indian heads of government at their tenth summit meeting (July 1989) in Grenada. Its primary thrust was to make CARICOM a common market in practice as well as in name, something that quite frankly had not been done when the organization was founded. The main accords for operationalizing these aspirations committed its members to taking the following steps: implementing by no later than January 1991 a comprehensive CET, a uniform standard for handling Rules of Origin trade questions, and a Harmonized Scheme of Fiscal Incentives; resuscitating the Caribbean Multilateral Clearing Facility (a mechanism for handling currency exchanges and payments and for extending credit that was established in 1976 and suspended its functions in 1983); eliminating practically all barriers to intraregional commerce by July 1991; and institutionalizing air-sea transport cooperation.[3] To help promote and facilitate attainment of these goals, the summit participants created the West Indian Commission. This blue-ribbon group, composed of seventeen Caribbean luminaries led by Sir Shridath Ramphal[4] and assured that it could pursue its work free of any governmental pressure, was asked to prepare a detailed report (including specific recommendations), to be presented at the July 1992 summit, on the necessary steps to be taken to assure greater internal cohesion as the region enters the twenty-first century.

The eleventh summit (August 1990) in Kingston, Jamaica, provided additional impetus to the Grand Anse blueprint. All the governments pledged, for instance, to enact legislation to assure that West Indians could travel freely (i.e., no passports required) within the region and to eliminate their work permit requirements for citizens of fellow CARICOM states. These two understandings laid the groundwork for satisfying one of the core criteria for a full-fledged common market—the unfettered movement therein of labor. Moreover, after some adjustments were made to allow the smaller countries a longer phase-in period, the conference reaffirmed January 1, 1991, as the deadline to begin applying the CET system. Finally, in a move indicative of the organization's interest in closer ties with the Hispanic mainland, Mexico and Venezuela were accorded official observer status within CARICOM. Also, participation was expanded by granting associate membership to the British Virgin Islands as well as the Turks and Caicos Islands,[5] although action on the Dominican Republic's application to upgrade its position from observer to full member was deferred because of lingering resentment over a dispute concerning its alleged violation of agreements regulating the export of Caribbean bananas to Europe.[6]

An aura of disorientation was to some degree evident at the twelfth CARICOM summit, which convened on St. Kitts in early July 1991. There were, to be sure, some concrete and positive steps taken. The organization continued, for example, to expand its scope by adding Anguilla and Colombia to its list of official observers, and a major advance in cooperation with Latin America transpired with the signing of an accord with Caracas that opened the way for West Indian exports to enjoy duty-free entry to Venezuelan markets. On the other hand, the U.S. Enterprise for the Americas Initiative (EAI), announced by George Bush's administration in June 1991, seemed to exert a disequilibrating impact on the process of setting CARICOM foreign policy priorities. In particular, the West Indian leaders seemed unsure as to whether they should place primary emphasis on developing their South-South relations in an effort to establish a broad hemispheric front as a prerequisite for subsequent EAI–related negotiations with Washington or concentrate on an immediate but essentially regional response to Bush's overtures. Ultimately they decided not to make any hard choices and instead to explore all their options. Thus, in addition to reconfirming the commitment to achieve the increasingly higher levels of internal integration called for in the 1989 Grand Anse Declaration,[7] the summit's final communiqué called for intensification of CARICOM–Latin American relations, maintenance of strong Lomé ties with the EC, greater efforts to promote developmental cooperation with Pacific Rim countries (e.g., Japan), and the conclusion of an EAI trade-investment framework agreement with the United States[8] (which, as noted below, was subsequently done). Basically, then, to use a gambling analogy, the CARICOM leaders tried to reduce their risks by covering all their bets and thereby buy the time needed to consider their alternatives more fully.

There is, of course, a basic duality to all this activity. From a purely regional perspective, the campaign to strengthen CARICOM can be seen as an effort to move as far as possible toward collective self-reliance. To do so demands that the West Indies go beyond a regime of multilateral cooperation to a much higher degree of economic-political unity. Realistically, however, the size-versus-viability issue that has always plagued the area, combined with the unique problems involved in trying to integrate island societies, places inevitable and rather severe limits on the process. In short, while there are substantial benefits to be gained that justify making the effort, it must be accepted that CARICOM's journey down the road to self-reliance is likely to be quite brief. Consequently it is in the larger international realm that the ramifications of greater unity will be most important, which leads within the context of postdependency politics to the following quick survey of possible trends for the foreseeable future.

The Established Dimensions of
CARICOM Postdependency Politics

Turning first to the NAM and G-77, it is highly likely that the G-77 will (at least in the short run) attract the most CARICOM attention. Historically, of course, it has tended to be the NAM that has received top postdependency priority from the West Indian community. But the Movement faces what might be termed an acute identity crisis as it enters the 1990s, the basic task being to redefine its international mission. When it first appeared on the scene the NAM had two main functions: to promote decolonization and to advance Third World political-security interests against a backdrop of intense superpower confrontationalism. Later, in the 1970s and 1980s, it added a third major thrust that revolved around strong advocacy of the NIEO as the most appropriate model for restructuring North-South economic relations. The problem is that these concerns may for the most part be irrelevant to the 1990s. Surely this is true of decolonization, for aside from the highly volatile Palestinian question (which does not, by the way, fit the usual anticolonial mold), there are very few remaining cases that arouse much Third World passion. Likewise, the Cold War's demise and the disintegration of the Soviet bloc render the Movement's commitment to proactive nonalignment somewhat anachronistic. Symbolic of this situation is the suggestion being heard from some quarters to remove the term *Third World* from the international glossary, since the bipolar system with which it was intimately associated no longer exists. North-South economic relations do remain a pressing matter, but the center of action here has shifted from NIEO–style macroconceptualizing within the NAM to the arena of highly specialized negotiations (e.g., the various GATT rounds) in which the G-77 normally represents LDC interests.

Essentially, then, there was a fairly clear-cut division of Third World labor in the decades preceding the 1990s that entailed a vigorous, high-profile role for the NAM and important, although somewhat inconspicuous responsibilities for the G-77. But the new configurations of power and issue-areas in the 1990s have in effect produced a status reversal, with the G-77 being perceived as the organization whose activities are most pertinent to contemporary Third World concerns. Accordingly, the CARICOM states can now be expected to utilize it more heavily than the NAM as a vehicle for pursuing their postdependency ambitions.

In contrast to the more or less business-as-usual atmosphere that has been suggested with regard to future West Indian participation in the NAM and G-77, the postdependency momentum that has been building on the Latin American front since the late 1980s seems likely to continue and perhaps even become more pronounced. Certainly most signs indicate that both the Anglophone and Hispanic areas are quite interested in expanding and deepening their ties. For example, subsequent to an August 1989 meeting between President Carlos Andrés Pérez of Venezuela and five CARICOM leaders (A.N.R. Robinson of Trinidad and Tobago, Erskine Sandiford of Barbados, Desmond Hoyte of Guyana, Michael Manley of Jamaica, and James Mitchell of St. Vincent and the Grenadines), a working group composed of West Indian, Venezuelan, and other Latin American officials was created. The group was directed to formulate detailed plans for cooperation in achieving mutual self-reliance in foodstuffs, exploring for mineral resources, developing strategies for joint exploitation of export markets, expanding interregional trade, sharing technology, and integrating Caribbean–Latin American communication and transportation systems. A much more dramatic development was the agreement between Venezuela and CARICOM signed at the organization's July 1991 summit in St. Kitts–Nevis whereby Caracas gave the West Indies unilateral duty-free access to its markets for five years (with the understanding that a reciprocal free trade regime would subsequently be arranged).[9] The thread tying all these as well as other similar activities together is the desire to bring the resulting increased levels of hemispheric unity into play in North-South economic negotiations (especially with the United States and, if necessary, NAFTA).

An important factor lending support to this scenario is the recent renaissance of democratic forces and processes throughout the Western Hemisphere. The CARICOM states, given their Westminster-style political culture, naturally have a greater affinity for countries that operate along pluralistic, western liberal lines. Conversely, they have always been rather leery about the advisability of serious joint ventures with the kind of military dictatorships and brutal oligarchies that too often in the past have dominated the Latin American political scene. Sometimes such aversion has been rooted in noble human rights principles, while in other instances it was probably more a matter of either not trusting the government to keep its word or believing that it would not be able to survive long enough to do so. In any case, in contrast to recent decades, these subjective considerations now appear to be clearly conducive to increased CARICOM–Latin American cooperation.

On a more pragmatic note, another development that should enhance the hemisphere's stock in West Indian eyes is Mexico's renewed interest in Caribbean affairs after several years of relative neglect in the late 1980s. This rejuvenation was plainly evident at the August 1989 CARICOM summit in Jamaica, where the Mexican delegation, led by President Carlos Salinas de Gortari (who was attending pursuant to his country's newly acquired observer status), lobbied vigorously for a West Indian agreement with Bancomex (Bank of Mexico) to promote trade and sought to establish the Mexico-CARICOM Mixed Commission as a major vehicle for interregional cooperation. Additional initiatives followed in 1990, including a Mexican offer to help Jamaica reduce its heavy foreign debt through a $30 million equity swap arrangement.[10] Beyond the obvious benefits in terms of trade and aid diversification that a strong Mexican connection could provide, its most important postdependency implications revolve around the possibility of Mexico's serving as a sympathetic broker for the CARICOM nations in whatever dealings they may have with NAFTA.

Combine all of these factors, and Latin America emerges as a particularly attractive arena for West Indian postdependency politics. There are, however, two considerations that could function to divert Hispanic attention from developing closer CARICOM ties within a larger context of increased stress on hemispheric South-South relations. The first concerns the economic crisis confronting numerous Latin countries, especially the massive foreign debts of such key players (to whom many look for integrative leadership) as Mexico, Venezuela, Brazil, and Argentina. The immense pressure, both exogenous and endogenous, to register some dramatic progress in resolving these problems could lead governments to focus on their bilateral North-South relations at the expense of other (i.e., South-South) dimensions of their international agendas. Certainly Mexico is being buffeted by such crosscurrents; it continues to display a strong penchant for hemispheric affairs, yet the exigencies of its difficulties tend to push it toward the waiting (and some would say suffocating) arms of the United States. The second issue, which to some degree flows directly from the first, involves the growing vitality of the privatization phenomenon. Traditionally the state has played a vanguard role in the Latin economies, thereby giving governments a substantial amount of leverage in structuring the commercial-financial aspects of their foreign relations. But as privatization proceeds, such power will gradually but inexorably begin to shift into the hands of the private sector, where the primary emphasis may very well be on collaboration with the industrialized North rather than on fostering South-South linkages. Undoubtedly these factors will complicate any CARICOM attempts to inject a vigorous Latin American thrust into its overall postdependency strategy. The prospective benefits involved, however, appear to justify a major effort nevertheless.

The dynamics of these hemispheric events must be viewed in conjunction with U.S. policy and its possible impact on them. Demanding special attention is President Bush's EAI, which was announced on June 27, 1991. The EAI incorporates elements of both the CBI and NAFTA into a grandiose plan of economic cooperation for the entire Western Hemisphere. David Lewis summarizes it: "The three-part EAI program includes an offer of trade negotiations that would lead to a Western Hemisphere free-trade zone; new private investment incentives, including a $300 million program of annual grants; and forgiveness of some loans owed to the U.S. government in order to bolster an effort to reduce commercial bank debt."[11] He then notes a few key provisions in each category, some examples being: in trade, short-term bilateral negotiations of free trade agreement "frameworks" and unilateral U.S. tariff cuts for Latin American countries as part of the Uruguay Round of GATT talks; in investment, a new lending program under the auspices of the Inter-American Development Bank (IDB) to promote privatization efforts as well as the liberalization of investment regimes and a $1.5 billion investment fund, managed by the IDB, to provide additional support for countries undertaking investment reforms; and in debt, a write-off of some U.S. development loans on a case-by-case basis and financial support to facilitate debt reduction agreements with commercial banks.[12]

Jamaica moved quickly to take advantage of these debt initiatives by reaching an accord on August 23, 1991, that canceled $217 million of the amount that Kingston owed under the U.S. PL 480 commodities supply (food) program and rescheduled the remaining $54 million on much easier terms.[13] Further relief came in mid-January 1992 when the Bush administration agreed to give Jamaica a six-year grace period on $47 million of its U.S. obligations, with repayment then to be made in eighteen semiannual instalments.[14]

Whether the EAI will succeed in stimulating significant economic progress remains to be seen, although a healthy dose of skepticism seems warranted. Such pessimism arises from the EAI's similarities to the CBI, and the CBI's mediocre developmental track record. Although the details may differ somewhat, the trade and investment proposals in the two programs are conceptually quite similar. Both offer trade concessions (the centerpiece being duty-free access or least a close facsimile thereof to the U.S. market) and aid packets linked to the implementation of reforms designed to guarantee a capitalist society highly receptive to foreign (read Yankee) investment. The EAI's truly distinctive element lies in its approach to the debt issue, which generates somewhat mixed feelings. Certainly Washington's willingness to abandon its previous insistence on full repayment is to be applauded. Critics, however, suggest that, whether it is openly stated or not, there exists within the overall EAI a close connection between debt reduction and an open-arms posture toward U.S. investors. Viewed from this perspective, debt relief (as well as trade preferences) can be seen less as an exercise in developmental assistance and more as a ploy to expedite penetration of, and perhaps ultimate control over, Caribbean–Latin American economies by the Colossus of the North. Or, to use a more harsh characterization, it could be said that what is being advanced is simply repackaged dependency.

Compounding the apprehension arising from these uncertainties is the concern in some quarters that the EAI may be incompatible with a South-South strategy of postdependency politics on a truly hemispheric scale. Specifically, it is feared that despite the EAI's image of multilateralism there may be a clear bias in the White House toward having individual countries deal directly with Washington to finalize the terms of their relationship with the United States. During 1990–1991, for example, the Bush administration launched separate free trade framework discussions with at least twelve hemispheric nations. Unlike the Lomé process, then, the EAI in these instances functioned to discourage rather than encourage collective North-South bargaining. The rejoinder could, of course, be made that Washington clearly demonstrated its commitment to group negotiations in July 1991 when it signed formal agreements accepting the thirteen CARICOM countries as a single bargaining unit within the EAI context. Skeptics, however, suggest that both scenarios are equally detrimental to the emergence of a broad-based counterdependency front, since each operates to drive a wedge between the West Indians and their Hispanic colleagues.[15]

The international stage is always, as the preceding material demonstrates, in a state of flux that poses both threats and opportunities as far as its actors and their interests are concerned. Perhaps nowhere is this axiom more likely to intersect with CARICOM's contemporary post-dependency prospects than in Europe. The proverbial Old World is, of course, a top-priority area for the West Indies because it is where they have been able (within the Lomé process) to wield counterdependency bargaining power most vigorously. Two European developments in particular have immense implications for the evolving CARICOM–EC relationship: the

1992 unification scenario; and the extraordinary structural changes occurring in Eastern Europe.

The phrase *Europe 1992* refers to an agreement called the Single European Act (SEA), which came into force on July 1, 1987, and set a deadline of December 31, 1992, for transforming the EC into a much more tightly integrated entity characterized by a single market. Initially all internal barriers to the free movement of goods, capital, and labor as well as to the provision of services will be removed. Subsequently, regulations governing technical, health, fiscal, and other similar matters will be standardized.[16] In essence, then, what has transpired is a significant step toward the dream of a truly unified Western Europe. It is, however, the trade ramifications that will be the most immediately apparent and will have the greatest international impact, for what will emerge from the SEA is a massive market of 320 million people accounting for approximately 20 percent of all global commerce. Although the tides radiating from this megabloc will undoubtedly wash the shores of practically all countries, they should run unusually strong in the West Indies because the EC already is a major customer for many of the region's exports. Among these items, notes Paul Sutton, "are sugar, bananas, and rum in agriculture; and alumina, bauxite, refined petroleum, and petroleum products in minerals. Singly or in combination these account for 80 percent or more of the exports to the EC for nine of CARICOM's 13 member states, while for several others they are the main source of foreign exchange and providers of employment."[17] The main concern for the CARICOM nations as well as the ACP Group in general is how the metamorphosis to Europe 1992 will affect their evolving economic relations with the EC, and especially future Lomé negotiations. The Lomé IV agreement, concluded in December 1989 and scheduled to run for ten years as opposed to the five-year life spans of the first three versions,[18] has been seen by some observers as a harbinger of the problems the SEA is likely to create for the West Indies. Anthony González, for instance, argues that it

> bore testimony to the erosion of traditional European commitments to protect the export markets of principal Caribbean commodities such as sugar and bananas. The European Community failed to . . . safeguard Caribbean export guarantees from the impact of Europe's market unification of 1992. The Caribbean's trade privileges with Europe are vanishing as the EC seeks to globalize its commercial ties with the developing world and establish a special trade relationship with Eastern Europe and the Mediterranean.[19]

It is, of course, possible that such aspects of the fourth convention were merely the outcome of hard-nosed bargaining on the EC's part that would have occurred in any case. In the real world, however, interconnectivity reigns supreme. Thus it must be assumed that the SEA–driven restructuring of the European market will inevitably have a spillover effect involving some reconfiguration of the EC's international economic relations. The key issue, at least from the perspective of CARICOM postdependency politics, is whether this process will ultimately enhance or diminish the prospects for the West Indies to make their own transition to controlled dependence. To carry out this assessment demands that one go beyond extrapolation based on a single variable such as Lomé IV to a more comprehensive cost-benefit (or threat-opportunity) analysis. The main points of the balance sheet that results from such an exercise in the crucial area of trade relations are summarized in Table 5.1. Clearly the trade picture is mixed, with the extremely tenuous situation prevailing in the vital manufacturing sector lending little comfort to the CARICOM states. Moreover, unforeseen circumstances could radically alter the equation. Overall, however, the projected opportunities seem sufficient to justify continued pursuit of the South-South option through Lomé or some other vehicle.

Table 5.1 Projected Impact of Europe 1992 on CARICOM–EEC Trade

Costs/Threats	Benefits/Opportunities
Bananas. Central American producers who can provide better quality at lower cost will gain increased access to the EC and probably shrink CARICOM's existing market share.	Sugar. Agreements will not be adversely affected. CARICOM will continue to receive guaranteed prices above the going world market rate.
Rum. West Indian quota will remain low, and CARICOM will probably face increased competition from European producers.	Manufactured goods. Prospects are favorable, but only if CARICOM producers can meet the stringent standardized technical requirements that will be applied.
Manufactured goods. Prospects are very unfavorable if CARICOM producers cannot meet the stringent standardized technical requirements that will be applied.	Tourism. Creation of unified service-marketing mechanisms and joint-venture operations, combined with a larger pool of potential visitors, should markedly increase tourist flows and hard currency receipts.
	Financial sector. Opportunity exists for CARICOM institutions to establish links with European counterparts whose growth potential is considerable, which means possible access to institutions with large pools of readily available capital.
	Cocoa and coffee. Uniform excise tax rates are expected to boost both demand and prices within the EEC.

Sources: Paul Sutton, "1992: The EEC and the Caribbean," *Hemisphere* 3, no. 1 (Fall 1990): 24–25; and Sahadeo Basdeo, "The Single European Act: A CARICOM Perspective," *Journal of Interamerican Studies and World Affairs* 32, no. 2 (Summer 1990):112–117.

Whatever problems it might cause, at least the Europe 1992 scenario is proceeding in an orderly fashion, and the CARICOM states had ample prior notice to allow them to begin to plan their responses. The turmoil in Eastern Europe is, however, a completely different story. Often no one really seems to be in control and hence it is difficult, if not impossible, to determine with any accuracy where events will lead. It is, in short, a situation that can make outside governments extremely uncomfortable, for even if they endorse in principle the changes that are occurring, they likewise prefer to have some advance warning so they can make the adjustments necessary to try to minimize any negative impact on their own interests. Unfortunately, the West Indies find themselves in an awkward position as they confront the Eastern Europe of the 1990s.

CARICOM's main concern is the nature of the evolving relationships, especially in the economic realm, between the two Europes, with the greatest anxiety centering on the possible implications thereof for the EC's general Caribbean policies and its attitude to the Lomé process (which is, of course, a key pillar of West Indian postdependency politics). Until very recently the Eastern Europeans were for the most part isolated from the international economy, particularly the market sector dominated by the highly industrialized Western countries. Most of their trade and aid activity took place within COMECON (Council for Mutual Economic Assistance, also known as CMEA), which was the Soviet bloc's counterpart of the EEC. Thus the Eastern Europeans' economic horizons were primarily defined by their ties to the USSR.[20] Now, however, with COMECON gone (it was formally dissolved on June 28, 1991), they are fervently courting the capitalist world, especially the Western Europeans. The former German Democratic Republic, commonly called East Germany, gained entry to the EC by virtue of German reunification. Other former COMECON nations would like to follow suit, although it is doubtful that any will be granted full membership in the near future. Associate status is, however, a possibility, particularly for countries such as Czechoslovakia and Hungary that are in relatively good economic health and have demonstrated an ability to effectively implement some market-oriented reforms. Indeed Budapest began experimenting with what came to be called "goulash communism"—a socialist system onto which were fused some aspects of a market economy—as early as the late 1960s.

Such developments could, at the very least, be expected to divert the attention of the EC governments away from North-South affairs, for it is an unwritten law of international relations that there is a strong positive correlation between the proximity of instability and a country's interest in it: the closer it is to one's frontiers, the higher its priority on one's agenda. It is not, however, the possibility of such temporary benign neglect that most worries the West Indies, but rather such potential long-term hazards as:

1. Drastically reduced flows of foreign aid funds and private investment into CARICOM and Third World nations that could result as EC governments reorient their developmental assistance programs toward Eastern Europe, and as the former Soviet bloc becomes increasingly attractive to western entrepreneurs. Such fears are reflected in Carl Stone's comments that

> the opening up of Eastern Europe with the unification of Germany and Western capitalist penetration of many countries formerly part of an insulated socialist bloc means that these new linkages are likely to be established with Western Europe at the expense of Third World linkages. The abundance of cheap, skilled, and relatively highly educated labour in these Eastern bloc countries will attract European capital as well as foster some immigration into Western Europe. This pattern has already begun to unfold. Both developments will be at the expense of Third World linkages.[21]

2. The EC could be less willing to extend trade preferences and other similar concessions to the LDCs, instead being inclined to employ the resources involved to expedite pan-European integration. Should this possibility materialize, Lomé's viability as a postdependency vehicle could be seriously jeopardized.

Counterbalancing these doomsday projections is a simple fact that has too often been overlooked: events in Eastern Europe have brought into the international marketplace a vast pool of new customers with demands that could very well be satisfied by the CARICOM states. Rum, sugar, tropical fruits, some seafood, and bauxite come immediately to mind as product lines in which the West Indies could be quite competitive in servicing East European needs. Add to the picture the opportunities that might exist for the Caribbean tourism industry, and the scene begins to look much brighter from a CARICOM perspective.

Moving beyond purely economic considerations, there may also be some counterdependency benefits to be realized. For example, diversification is a crucial aspect of postdependency politics. However, a CARICOM diversification strategy that included the Soviet bloc was not very realistic when the Cold War was still raging, the primary reason being that the risks of U.S. retaliation were too great. The fate of Grenada's New Jewel Revolution (as well as the Sandinista experience in Nicaragua) stands as vivid evidence of the danger involved in arousing Washington's ire by attempting to establish close, cooperative relations with the socialist camp. But now the Eastern Europeans are, in a sense, simply faces in the international crowd, and hence having cordial ties with them is politically and ideologically inconsequential as far as the United States is concerned. Thus, by adding to the list of potential diversification candidates, changes in Eastern Europe have in effect presented the West Indies with new opportunities to expand the scope of their postdependency politics.

The possibility of incorporating former COMECON states into the EC framework can be seen in a similar light. The more closely associated with the EC the Kremlin's old allies may become, the greater the probability that they likewise might be drawn into the Lomé process. This would mean that the CARICOM nations and their ACP partners would be in a position to bring their collective bargaining power to bear on a larger scale by negotiating developmental agreements that would apply more broadly than before (i.e., to the previous EC contingent plus any new Eastern European participants). From this viewpoint, then, any move to open the EC to Eastern Europe would represent a postdependency asset to the CARICOM states, since it would increase the number of developed countries committed to North-South collective bargaining and would enhance the West Indies' chances to attain much more favorable terms for their Eastern European relations than otherwise might be the case.

In the final analysis, then, Europe appears to hold exciting prospects for CARICOM postdependency politics despite the potential pitfalls involved. The West Indians will, however, have to maintain extreme vigilance to assure that the advantages they have worked so hard to gain in their relations with Western Europe are not lost or seriously diluted in the complex and sometimes chaotic enterprise of building a radically new Europe.

Untapped Dimensions of CARICOM Postdependency Politics

Winston Churchill once said that the Soviet Union is a "riddle wrapped in a mystery inside an enigma." Without pushing the analogy too far, this description could to some degree apply to its current status within the evolving dynamics of CARICOM postdependency politics. Theoretically the former USSR presents many of the same prospects (and perhaps problems) as do the Eastern European states. Realistically, however, it seems much more accurate to characterize it as being rather far removed from the mainstream of West Indian affairs.

Traditionally the Kremlin has displayed minimal interest in the island Caribbean, with the exception of Cuba, and there is little to suggest that this posture is likely to change dramatically anytime in the near future. This prediction is based on two interrelated factors: Moscow's well-established Havana connection; and its perception of the CARICOM region as essentially irrelevant to the solution of its daunting domestic problems.

Despite fierce criticism of the Kremlin's relationship with Cuba (especially the large amounts of developmental assistance that Moscow has provided) from some elements within the former Soviet Communist Party and the society at large,[22] the two countries have not totally disengaged. The nature of their ties has, of course, changed dramatically, especially since Mikhail Gorbachev was displaced by Boris Yeltsin. The previously massive flow of Soviet aid has almost completely dried up, and trade is now based on market prices paid in hard currency (such terms being extremely disadvantageous to Havana). Nevertheless, recognizing that they simply cannot afford to lose their markets within the former eastern bloc, the Fidelistas have been making major efforts to adjust to these political-economic realities by negotiating new commercial agreements. Assuming that Cuba will be successful in these endeavors and therefore will continue to be Russia's primary supplier of many of the items that are staples on the West Indian export list (e.g., rum, sugar, tropical fruits, some seafoods), Moscow seems to have little to offer the CARICOM nations in terms of trade diversification.

Tourism prospects likewise appear to be rather bleak. The Anglophone states are already worried that Cuba's crash program to rebuild its tourist infrastructure and its renewed emphasis on promoting itself as a vacation center will once again propel it to the forefront of the Caribbean industry. Indeed the West Indies are beginning to feel the heat of increased Cuban competition in the lucrative Canadian and Western European markets (although the grand prize—the United States—remains closed to Havana). Combining such considerations with the fact that Cuba has much more experience in dealing with an Eastern European clientele leads to the conclusion that the opportunities for CARICOM to make any significant breakthroughs in Russian tourism are not particularly promising.

The West Indian position seems to be equally weak in the main areas where the Kremlin is looking abroad for help—investment capital, manufactured goods, and high-technology products and services. In each instance the CARICOM countries would in all probability be very much overshadowed by the United States, the EC, or the Asian powerhouses. Moscow, recognizing that any contribution that the West Indies might be able to make would be minuscule compared to its demands, is not likely to place much importance on cultivating a CARICOM connection. Or, to put it more bluntly, the Kremlin knows that the solution to its massive problems demands access to the resources controlled by the giants of the international community, which in practice translates into rather crass indifference toward the Lilliputians of the world. It would not, therefore, seem advisable for the West Indies to put much stock in Russia as a potential arena for practicing postdependency politics.

Looming prominently in the eyes of practically every Third World country interested in counterdependency diversification is Japan. Indeed even many developed nations who are experiencing some economic difficulties have, figuratively or literally, made the pilgrimage to Tokyo hoping to find a panacea for their ills. Thus it should hardly be surprising that similar sentiments can be found in the West Indies.

Historically commercial ties between the CARICOM region and Japan have been minimal, although the general trend has been upward in recent years.[23] Even so, as demonstrated in Table 5.2, Japan does not rank particularly high, especially as a market for West Indian exports, in the pantheon of CARICOM's highly industrialized trading partners. Likewise, the West Indies have not attracted significant amounts of Japanese developmental aid. In 1988, for example, all the independent CARICOM countries received some assistance, the largest amounts going to Jamaica ($5.62 million dollars) and Guyana ($2 million dollars). Yet on a proportional basis, this twelve-nation package represented only slightly over one-tenth of 1 percent of Tokyo's total foreign aid program.

Table 5.2 Japanese–West Indian Trade, 1988 (in Millions of U.S. Dollars)

	Exports to Japan	Partner Rank[a]	Imports from Japan	Partner Rank[a]
Bahamas	34.90	3	265.6	2
Barbados	1.30	5	31.7	4
Belize	0.80	5	21.6	3
Dominica	2.00	5	4.8	2
Grenada	.15	*	4.0	3
Guyana	6.50	*	12.8	3
Jamaica	14.90	*	46.2	4
St. Vincent	.97	5	7.2	3
Trinidad and Tobago	8.10	*	58.5	4

Sources: International Monetary Fund, *Direction of Trade Statistics Yearbook 1989* (Washington, DC: IMF, 1989); Jacqueline Braveboy-Wagner, "Caribbean Foreign Relations: Current State and Prospects for Diversification" (paper presented at the sixteenth International Congress of the Latin American Studies Association, Washington, DC, April 4–6, 1991).

[a]Japan's rank among industrial countries. An asterisk denotes ranking lower than fifth.

If we look to the future rather than the past, there are several important factors beyond Japan's vast investment resources and its market potential that could make it particularly attractive to LDCs surveying the prospects for postdependency diversification in the industrialized North. Among the most salient as far as the West Indies are concerned are

- An accommodating stance on the issue of technology transfers

  Japanese firms investing in Third World areas recognize that their hosts want an infusion of the most advanced technology available and, unlike their counterparts in many other industrialized nations, accept concessions to such desires as an unavoidable cost of doing business.

- Japanese willingness to enter joint ventures as junior partners

  Many MNCs, especially those based in the United States, insist on having a majority interest in their overseas subsidiaries, which is inconsistent with the key postdependency principle that LDCs must achieve effective sovereignty and that to do so requires that they avoid external penetration or control of their affairs. The Japanese position, on the other hand, is much more attuned to Third World aspirations to make the transition to controlled dependence.

- Tokyo, under pressure to recycle the country's large trade surplus, generally offers foreign aid on terms much more favorable than those of many other industrialized nations

- The Japanese government has been a leader among the developed states in supporting debt relief for the LDCs

The common thread running through all the points listed above is their potential compatibility with Third World postdependency politics. Prudence, therefore, seems to suggest that the CARICOM Secretariat take prompt action, either on its own or preferably in concert with other developing countries, to explore the opportunities to make progress toward controlled dependence that a Japanese linkage might offer.

Conclusion

Political forecasting is always risky, especially in the tumultuous sphere of international relations, where circumstances and therefore government policy can change very rapidly. The enterprise becomes even more problematical when dealing with a topic such as postdependency politics wherein the historical record is rather sparse with regard to carefully orchestrated experiments that might provide some insight into the practical dynamics of the process. With such caveats in mind, we can summarize the areas of greatest potential for future CARICOM initiatives in pursuit of controlled dependence (Table 5.3). The NAFTA entry in Table 5.3 obviously must be considered tentative until such a free trade agreement begins to become fully operative. But if and when it does, the hemispheric countries will have to respond and, given the awesome concentration of economic power that the

Table 5.3 CARICOM Postdependency Politics: High-Potential Areas

South-South diversification	Latin America
North-South diversification	Japan[a] Eastern Europe
North-South collective bargaining	Lomé Process[b] Group of 77 CARICOM–Latin America/NAFTA (?)

[a]Japan has the greater postdependency potential.
[b]The Lomé process offers the greatest postdependency potential.

proposed free trade area would represent, logic seems to dictate a multilateral rather than a bilateral approach as the most appropriate. Hence it would probably be wise for CARICOM to consider some counterinitiatives based on South-South postdependency collaboration with its Latin American neighbors in order to maximize its bargaining power.

Yet whatever the specific moves that the CARICOM states might take to deal with such immediate problems as Europe 1992 and the specter of NAFTA, it is still unclear whether they will be able to make and especially to consolidate a transition to controlled dependence. Pessimists—and they are many—will continue to debunk the idea as absurd and totally out of touch with reality. And they may very well be proved correct, for the old size-versus-viability issue will continue to haunt the region and perhaps psychologically debilitate it to the point where fatalistic resignation overpowers the will to struggle.

At this point, however, some historical perspective is needed. The year 1992 marks the Columbian quincentennial. For almost that entire five-hundred-year span the West Indies were ravaged in one form or another by western imperialism. Only in the last thirty years have they had any chance to exert some significant control over their destinies, and, considering the constraints under which they have had to operate, they seem to have done rather well. The progress that has been made in the field of regional integration, while clearly not as much as many had hoped for, is still solid when measured against the experiences of other areas (e.g., Europe, Latin America, and even the early United States) where the actors involved enjoyed at least formal sovereignty for much longer than have CARICOM's members. Even more impressive is the vanguard role played in helping to organize the ACP Group and to launch the Lomé process. Thus, as West Indians stand on the threshold of the twenty-first century, the resilience and tenacity that they have frequently displayed in the face of adversity will once again be tested as they confront the challenges of modern postdependency politics.

Notes

1. Anthony Bryan, "The New International Relations Agenda: Is the Commonwealth Caribbean Ready for the 1990s?" *Caribbean Affairs* 2, no. 4 (October–December 1989): 53–54.

2. Adopting a pessimistic perspective on NAFTA's potential impact on the CARICOM area, Andrés Serbín ("The Caribbean: Myths and Realities for the 1990s," *Journal of Interamerican Studies and World Affairs* 32, no. 2 [Summer 1990]: 135) suggests that

> given the present trends towards economic blocs in general, and the consolidation of a (US-dominated) North American bloc in particular, it is probable that the insular Caribbean will increasingly become absorbed into this US sphere of influence. This suggests an increased US presence in the English-speaking Caribbean at the political and military levels; while the Caribbean Basin Initiatives (both I and II) will be its effective instruments at the economic level, with Puerto Rico as the key player.

3. This information comes from Sahadeo Basdeo, "Economic Imperatives for Caribbean Foreign Policy in the 21st Century," *Caribbean Affairs* 2, no. 4 (October–December 1989): 83–84.

4. The members appointed to the West Indian Commission were Dame Nita Barrow (patron; governor-general of Barbados); Sir Shridath Ramphal (chair; chancellor of the Universities of the West Indies and Guyana); Alister McIntyre (vice-chair; vice-chancellor of the University of the West Indies); Leonard Archer (former president of the Caribbean Congress of Labor); Dr. Vaughan Lewis (director-general, OECS); William Demas (governor, Central Bank of Trinidad and Tobago); Sandra Mason (magistrate); Howard Fergus (resident tutor, UWI); Gillian Nanton (economist); Marshall Hall (managing director, Jamaica Banana Producers); the Rev. Allan Kirton (general secretary, Caribbean Conference of Churches); Roderick Rainford (secretary-general, CARICOM); Neville Trotz (science advisor, Commonwealth Secretariat); Frank Rampersad (coordinator, Caribbean Economic Conference); Rex Nettleford (pro-vice-chancellor, UWI); and Don Brice (director-general, Commission's Secretariat).

5. See the following issues of *Latin American Regional Reports: Caribbean Report:* August 30, 1990, p. 1; October 4, 1990, p. 1; and December 13, 1990, p. 1.

6. For details, see Andrés Serbín, "The CARICOM States and the Group of Three: A New Partnership Between Latin America and the Non-Hispanic Caribbean?" (paper presented at the sixteenth International Congress of the Latin American Studies Association, Washington, DC, April 4–6, 1991), pp. 12–15. This incident was only one in a series of controversies spanning a number of years that had generated deep suspicion in CARICOM circles that the Dominican Republic could not be relied on to fulfill its commitments.

7. The sincerity of this commitment subsequently came under fire from a number of critics. For example, Sir Shridath Ramphal (chair of the West Indian Commission) complained that CARICOM was moving much too slowly with regard

to integration and publicly chastised West Indian leaders for what he considered to be their failure to make significant progress on the immediate action programs agreed upon at the St. Kitts summit. For details, see "Caricom Ties with Central America: Ramphal Complains About 'Snail's Pace' of Integration," *Latin American Regional Reports: Caribbean Report* (February 27, 1992), 4–5.

8. The full text can be found in CARICOM Secretariat, "Communiqué," *Caribbean Affairs* 4, no. 3 (July–September 1991): 112–122. Two other items of interest in this source regarding the St. Kitts summit are CARICOM Secretariat, "Preliminary Report of CARICOM on Enterprise for the Americas Initiative," pp. 68–72; and the West Indian Commission, "Towards a Vision of the Future: Progress Report of the Work of the West Indian Commission," pp. 102–111.

9. Reported in "Trade Pact with Venezuela at Summit a Step Towards 'Widening' CARICOM," *Latin American Regional Reports: Caribbean Report* (July 25, 1991): 2. For the text of the address by Venezuela's president to the St. Kitts–Nevis summit, see Carlos Andrés Pérez, "The Strengthening of the Venezuelan/CARICOM Relationship," *Caribbean Affairs* 4, no. 3 (July–September 1991): 8–13. The text of the proposed agreement can be found in "The Venezuelan Free Trade Agreement Proposal for CARICOM," printed in the same issue of *Caribbean Affairs,* 14–23.

10. The information here comes from *Caribbean Affairs* 4, no. 3 (July–September 1991): 20–21.

11. David E. Lewis, "Political Hegemony and Economic Crisis: The Challenges for U.S. Foreign Policy in the Caribbean" (paper presented at the sixteenth International Congress of the Latin American Studies Association, Washington, DC, April 4–6, 1991), p. 3.

12. Ibid., pp. 3–4.

13. "Jamaica's Debt Cut by U.S.," *New York Times* (August 24, 1991), p. 33.

14. "Jamaica/US Reschedules Debt," *Latin American Regional Reports: Caribbean Report* (February 27, 1992): 5. This article also notes that Kingston's outstanding general debt to the United States is approximately $750 million, which means that the $47 million rescheduled represented only 6.3 percent of the total owed.

15. This development is reported in "Caricom–US Agreement Paves Way for 'Dynamic' and 'Growth-Inducing' Ties," *Latin American Regional Reports: Caribbean Report* (August 29, 1991): 1. The agreement established a CARICOM–U.S. council to monitor trade and investment relations, to promote open markets between the two parties, and to negotiate whatever implementing mechanisms are necessary. Washington stressed that CARICOM was the largest group of nations to enter into such an arrangement since the EAI was announced in June 1990.

16. Some general discussions and analyses of Europe 1992 are Michael Davenport, *Europe 1992 and the Developing World* (London: Overseas Development Council, 1991); Michael A. Silva and Bertil Sjogren, *Europe 1992 and the New World Power Game* (New York: John Wiley and Sons, 1990); and Ernest Wistrich, *After 1992: The United States of Europe* (London: Routledge, 1990).

17. Paul Sutton, "1992: The EC and the Caribbean," *Hemisphere* 3, no. 1 (Fall 1990): 24.

18. A summary of Lomé IV's provisions is in CARICOM Secretariat, "CARICOM Secretariat Reports on Lomé IV and Women's Legislation," *Caribbean Affairs* 4, no. 3 (July–September 1991): 85–88. Although this report contains no analysis or evaluation of Lomé IV, the data presented certainly indicate that the Caribbean lost some ground compared to the previous agreement. For example, Lomé III provided approximately 54 million ECU (European Currency Units) for regional

projects, while the Lomé IV figure is 90 million ECU. Remember, however, that Lomé IV is a ten-year plan, which means that its five-year average of 45 million ECU is below the Lomé III five-year total of 54 million ECU. Moreover, the Lomé IV allocation will in effect be spread more thinly across the region because two additional Caribbean countries—Haiti and the Dominican Republic—became parties to the most recent agreement.

19. Anthony P. González, "The View from the Caribbean," *Hemisphere* 3, no. 1 (Fall 1990): 26–27.

20. Among the more general surveys of COMECON are William V. Wallace and Roger A. Clark, *COMECON, Trade, and the West* (London: Pinter, 1986); Vladimir Sobell, *The Red Market: Industrial Co-Operation and Specialization in COMECON* (Aldershot, Hants, Eng.: Gower, 1984); and Giuseppe Schiavone, *The Institutions of COMECON* (New York: Holmes and Meier, 1981).

21. Carl Stone, "A Unified Regional European Market and Its Implications Challenges the Caribbean," *Caribbean Affairs* 3, no. 3 (July–September 1990): 61.

22. The reform-oriented *Moscow News* has been one of the most vociferous sources of Russian criticism of Cuba, castigating Castro for his reluctance to embrace the concepts of *glasnost* and *perestroika,* as well as serving as one of the main fora for those who want the Kremlin to distance itself from, if not sever practically all of its relations with, the island. Even some "old establishment" publications have called for a major reassessment of Moscow's Havana connection. For example, the *Miami Herald* (October 3, 1990) reported that *Pravda,* the official paper of the USSR's Communist Party, stated in an October 2, 1990, editorial that it was time to rethink the country's relationship with Cuba and particularly to alter it from one of "philanthropy to collaboration."

23. Most of the material presented here concerning Japan is based on the work of Jacqueline Braveboy-Wagner, who is probably the leading authority on CARICOM-Japanese relations. The specific sources used for this section are her "Japan and the Caribbean: Linkages and Possibilities," *Caribbean Affairs* 2, no. 4 (October–December 1989): 109–122; and "Caribbean Foreign Relations: Current State and Prospects for Diversification" (paper presented at the sixteenth International Congress of the Latin American Studies Association, Washington, DC, April 4–6, 1991).

Index

About the Book and Author

This book seeks to examine, in both theoretical and practical terms, the generally unexplored waters of postdependency politics. Erisman argues that the option of South-South relations can be a viable way for a developing country to move beyond dependency by acquiring either enough bargaining power to exert some control over the terms of its dependent North-South relations or the maneuvering space necessary to minimize its exposure to any single foreign source of influence. Although focusing on the South-South initiatives of the West Indian CARICOM states, he sheds light as well on the evolving role of small states in general in the contemporary international system.

H. Michael Erisman is department head and professor of political science at Indiana State University, Terre Haute. His main fields of interest are U.S. policies on Latin America, transnationalism and political economy in the Caribbean Basin, and Cuban foreign affairs. He is the author of *Cuba's International Relations: The Anatomy of a Nationalistic Foreign Policy*. He edited *The Caribbean Challenge: U.S. Policy in a Volatile Region* and co-edited, with John Martz, *Colossus Challenged: The Struggle for Caribbean Influence* and, with John Kirk, *Cuban Foreign Policy Confronts a New International Order*. He has written numerous journal articles and book chapters focusing on Caribbean international affairs in general and Cuban foreign policy in particular.

The Council for the International Exchange of Scholars awarded him a Senior Fulbright Fellowship in 1985–1986 at the Institute of International Relations of the University of the West Indies (St. Augustine, Trinidad). Much of the field research incorporated into this book was undertaken in conjunction with that fellowship. His current research agenda involves projects dealing with U.S.–Cuban relations and Havana's evolving relations with countries of the Far East.